# Alzheimer's Disease

# Other Books of Related Interest

# Alzheimer's Disease

Adela Soliz, *Book Editor*

Bruce Glassman, *Vice President*
Bonnie Szumski, *Publisher*
Helen Cothran, *Managing Editor*
David M. Haugen, *Series Editor*

## Contemporary Issues
## Companion

**GREENHAVEN PRESS**
An imprint of Thomson Gale, a part of The Thomson Corporation

**THOMSON**
**GALE**

Detroit • New York • San Francisco • San Diego • New Haven, Conn.
Waterville, Maine • London • Munich

*For more information, contact*
Greenhaven Press
27500 Drake Rd.
Farmington Hills, MI 48331-3535
Or you can visit our Internet site at http://www.gale.com

| LIBRARY OF CONGRESS CATALOGING-IN-PUBLICATION DATA |
| --- |
| Alzheimer's disease / Adela Soliz, book editor. |
| p. cm. — (Contemporary issues companion) |
| Includes bibliographical references and index. |
| ISBN 0-7377-2442-0 (lib. : alk. paper) — ISBN 0-7377-2443-9 (pbk. : alk. paper) |
| 1. Alzheimer's disease—Popular works. I. Soliz, Adela. II. Series. |
| RC523.2A443 2006 |
| 616.8'31—dc22                                             2005046346 |

# CONTENTS

# FOREWORD

In the news, on the streets, and in neighborhoods, individuals are confronted with a variety of social problems. Such problems may affect people directly: A young woman may struggle with depression, suspect a friend of having bulimia, or watch a loved one battle cancer. And even the issues that do not directly affect her private life—such as religious cults, domestic violence, or legalized gambling—still impact the larger society in which she lives. Discovering and analyzing the complexities of issues that encompass communal and societal realms as well as the world of personal experience is a valuable educational goal in the modern world.

Effectively addressing social problems requires familiarity with a constantly changing stream of data. Becoming well informed about today's controversies is an intricate process that often involves reading myriad primary and secondary sources, analyzing political debates, weighing various experts' opinions—even listening to firsthand accounts of those directly affected by the issue. For students and general observers, this can be a daunting task because of the sheer volume of information available in books, periodicals, on the evening news, and on the Internet. Researching the consequences of legalized gambling, for example, might entail sifting through congressional testimony on gambling's societal effects, examining private studies on Indian gaming, perusing numerous websites devoted to Internet betting, and reading essays written by lottery winners as well as interviews with recovering compulsive gamblers. Obtaining valuable information can be time-consuming—since it often requires researchers to pore over numerous documents and commentaries before discovering a source relevant to their particular investigation.

Greenhaven's Contemporary Issues Companion series seeks to assist this process of research by providing readers with useful and pertinent information about today's complex issues. Each volume in this anthology series focuses on a topic of current interest, presenting informative and thought-provoking selections written from a wide variety of viewpoints. The readings selected by the editors include such diverse sources as personal accounts and case studies, pertinent factual and statistical articles, and relevant commentaries and overviews. This diversity of sources and views, found in every Contemporary Issues Companion, offers readers a broad perspective in one convenient volume.

In addition, each title in the Contemporary Issues Companion series is designed especially for young adults. The selections included in every volume are chosen for their accessibility and are expertly edited in consideration of both the reading and comprehension levels of the audience. The structure of the anthologies also enhances accessibility. An introductory essay places each issue in context and provides helpful facts such as historical background or current statistics and legislation that pertain to the topic. The chapters that follow organize the material and focus on specific aspects of the book's topic. Every essay is introduced by a brief summary of its main points and biographical information about the author. These summaries aid in comprehension and can also serve to direct readers to material of immediate interest and need. Finally, a comprehensive index allows readers to efficiently scan and locate content.

The Contemporary Issues Companion series is an ideal launching point for research on a particular topic. Each anthology in the series is composed of readings taken from an extensive gamut of resources, including periodicals, newspapers, books, government documents, the publications of private and public organizations, and Internet websites. In these volumes, readers will find factual support suitable for use in reports, debates, speeches, and research papers. The anthologies also facilitate further research, featuring a book and periodical bibliography and a list of organizations to contact for additional information.

A perfect resource for both students and the general reader, Greenhaven's Contemporary Issues Companion series is sure to be a valued source of current, readable information on social problems that interest young adults. It is the editors' hope that readers will find the Contemporary Issues Companion series useful as a starting point to formulate their own opinions about and answers to the complex issues of the present day.

# INTRODUCTION

Alzheimer's is a disease in which plaque forms in the brain, causing dementia and, eventually, death. Dementia is defined as a condition of deteriorating mentality often accompanied by emotional apathy. Those who suffer from Alzheimer's forget the people and places they knew well as their minds deteriorate. They become disoriented and tend to wander, not recognizing where they are. Although Alzheimer's is usually considered a disease of the elderly, early-onset Alzheimer's can strike people when they are in their thirties, though this is exceedingly rare. Only 6 to 8 percent of people who have Alzheimer's develop symptoms before the age of sixty-five. Genetic links to Alzheimer's disease have been discovered, but many other potential causes of the disease are also under investigation, including head trauma, aluminum intake, and depression. Although there are drugs and therapies that alleviate some of the symptoms of Alzheimer's, there is no known cure. The only way to definitely diagnose the disease is to perform an autopsy after a patient dies.

An increasing number of people in the United States have a family member or friend who has been struck with Alzheimer's disease. It is unclear, however, whether the number of people with the disease has escalated recently or if physicians are now better able to recognize the symptoms of Alzheimer's and make more diagnoses. In either case, the number of people with Alzheimer's is growing. Jane Weaver, writing for MSNBC, states, "Experts warn that a potentially devastating Alzheimer's epidemic is looming. There are 4.5 million people in the United States currently living with Alzheimer's disease, and the number is expected to rise to as many as 16 million by 2050, according to the National Institutes of Health."

The growing number of Alzheimer's patients in the United States has caused medical researchers to shift their focus from efforts to treat Alzheimer's patients to efforts to prevent the disease. As journalist Mayrav Saar explains in an article in the *Orange County Register*, "For years, Alzheimer's disease research centered around treating the ill: reducing plaques in the brain, reversing the deterioration that had already set in. But as baby boomers approach the age when Alzheimer's begins, the focus has shifted from the ill to those who could become ill—from treatment to prevention." Finding ways to prevent Alzheimer's would save patients and their families from the anguish that inevitably accompanies the devastating illness as well as the exorbitant hospital and nursing home bills. It would also alleviate the stress-related health problems that many family and professional caregivers experience while caring for Alzheimer's patients.

Scientists are exploring a number of approaches to preventing Alzheimer's disease. One of these is the attempt to develop a gene-based vaccine for the disease. As the January 8, 2005, issue of *Obesity, Fitness, and Wellness Week* states, scientists searching for an Alzheimer's vaccine have moved away from looking for protein-based vaccines and have started investigating the possibility of creating a gene-based vaccine. The researchers are seeking to develop an Alzheimer's vaccine that will not cause the harmful side effects produced by protein-based vaccines. The newsletter states, "UT [University of Texas] Southwestern researchers have created a gene-based vaccine aimed at stimulating the immune systems of mice to potentially fight off plaque-causing amyloid protein in the brain." The researchers hope to begin human trials of the gene vaccine by 2007. However, it could be many years before an effective vaccine is available to the public.

While a vaccine for Alzheimer's has not yet been developed, current research suggests that people may reduce their odds of developing Alzheimer's by making immediate changes in their exercise and eating habits. A 2003 report by the Alzheimer's Disease Education and Referral Center notes that "exercise appears to recruit brain processes that contribute to cognitive functioning and to activate cellular mechanisms that protect the brain and promote its repair." The *Times Argus* reported on an additional study by scientists at the University of Chicago, who found that "the reason that mentally and physically active people tend to have less Alzheimer's disease may be that education and exercise supercharge a broad set of genes involved in building a healthier brain." The scientists believe that taking simple measures to maintain a healthy body, such as increasing exercise, may make an important contribution in preventing dementia.

Maintaining a healthy body weight may also help to prevent the development of Alzheimer's. A study published by the University Hospital of Göteborg, Sweden, in 2003 suggests that there is a link between obesity and Alzheimer's disease. The researchers conducted an eighteen-year study of 226 women and 166 men who were seventy or older and considered to be healthy. The women who were overweight at the beginning of the study had a greater likelihood of developing Alzheimer's than the women of normal weight. The researchers reported that for every 1.0 percent increase in the body mass index of the women, the risk of developing Alzheimer's rose by 36 percent. However, the researchers did not find the same link with the male participants.

In the past few years, research has revealed that there may also be a strong link between the development of heart disease and Alzheimer's, and that therefore the prevention of heart disease may also help to prevent Alzheimer's. The Honolulu-Asia Aging study showed that middle-aged Japanese men with diastolic blood pressure higher than 90 had a risk of developing dementia that was five times greater than those men whose diastolic pressure fell in the 80 to 89 range. In addition, other cardiac risk factors including smoking, atherosclerosis (hardening of the arteries), and high cholesterol have been implicated in Alzheimer's disease. These findings suggest that if people adopt lifestyles that support healthy hearts, they will also be working to prevent dementia.

As increasing numbers of Americans develop Alzheimer's, more money is being spent on research to treat and prevent it. In an article for the *Los Angeles Times*, journalist Jia Lynn Yang writes, "Ten years ago [in 1994]—about the time [President Ronald] Reagan was diagnosed with the disease—the government was committing about $300 million a year to research. . . . Funding for Alzheimer's research for the fiscal year 2005 is estimated at $700 million." As a result of this increased government funding, a wider variety of research projects can be pursued, offering some hope that the potential epidemic can be avoided. However, although many pharmaceutical companies are searching for vaccines and treatments for Alzheimer's, it could be at least fifteen years before any drug becomes available to the public. Therefore, experts suggest that the most immediate way to reduce the threat of the disease is for people to make lifestyle changes that promote a healthy body and brain, including eating low-fat foods, exercising, and giving up smoking. Although none of these health measures guarantees that a person will not develop Alzheimer's, it makes sense to take every possible step to avoid the risk of this debilitating and fatal illness.

# CHAPTER 1

# WHAT IS ALZHEIMER'S DISEASE?

Contemporary Issues
Companion

# FACTS ABOUT ALZHEIMER'S DISEASE

National Institute on Aging

The following selection is an excerpt from a pamphlet by the Alzheimer's Disease Education and Referral (ADEAR) Center, a service of the National Institute on Aging. ADEAR was created by Congress in 1990 to serve as a comprehensive information source about Alzheimer's for health care professionals, patients, and caregivers. The excerpt briefly describes Alzheimer's disease and its causes, which are not yet fully understood. According to ADEAR, several factors, including age, genetics, and diet, may contribute to the development of the disease. The selection also discusses the symptoms of Alzheimer's, which involve a steady deterioration of the memory. In addition, the article provides an introduction to how the disease is diagnosed, noting that the only definitive way to determine if someone has Alzheimer's is to examine his or her brain tissue, which can only be done after death.

Dementia is a brain disorder that seriously affects a person's ability to carry out daily activities. The most common form of dementia among older people is Alzheimer's disease (AD), which involves the parts of the brain that control thought, memory, and language. Although scientists are learning more every day, right now they still do not know what causes AD, and there is no cure.

Scientists think that as many as 4.5 million Americans suffer from AD. The disease usually begins after age 60, and risk goes up with age. While younger people also may get AD, it is much less common. About 5 percent of men and women ages 65 to 74 have AD, and nearly half of those age 85 and older may have the disease. It is important to note, however, that AD is not a normal part of aging.

AD is named after Dr. Alois Alzheimer, a German doctor. In 1906, Dr. Alzheimer noticed changes in the brain tissue of a woman who had died of an unusual mental illness. He found abnormal clumps (now called amyloid plaques) and tangled bundles of fibers (now

National Institute on Aging, "Alzheimer's Fact Sheet," www.alzheimers.org, 2004. Copyright © 2004 by Alzheimer's Disease Education and Referral (ADEAR) Center. Reproduced by permission.

called neurofibrillary tangles). Today, these plaques and tangles in the brain are considered signs of AD.

Scientists also have found other brain changes in people with AD. Nerve cells die in areas of the brain that are vital to memory and other mental abilities. There also are lower levels of some of the chemicals in the brain that carry messages back and forth between nerve cells. AD may impair thinking and memory by disrupting these messages.

## What Causes AD?

Scientists do not yet fully understand what causes AD. There probably is not one single cause, but several factors that affect each person differently. Age is the most important known risk factor for AD. The number of people with the disease doubles every 5 years beyond age 65.

Family history is another risk factor. Scientists believe that genetics may play a role in many AD cases. For example, familial AD, a rare form of AD that usually occurs between the ages of 30 and 60, is inherited. The more common form of AD is known as late-onset. It occurs later in life, and no obvious inheritance pattern is seen. However, several risk factor genes may interact with each other to cause the disease. The only risk factor gene identified so far for late-onset AD, is a gene that makes one form of a protein called apolipoprotein E (ApoE). Everyone has ApoE, which helps carry cholesterol in the blood. It is likely that other genes also may increase the risk of AD or protect against AD, but they remain to be discovered. The National Institute on Aging (NIA), part of the National Institutes of Health, is sponsoring the AD Genetics Study to recruit families with AD to learn more about risk factor genes. To participate in this study, families should contact the National Cell Repository for AD toll-free at 1-800-526-2839. Information may also be requested through their website: http://ncrad.iu.edu.

Scientists still need to learn a lot more about what causes AD. In addition to genetics and ApoE, they are studying education, diet, and environment to learn what role they might play in the development of this disease. Scientists are finding increasing evidence that some of the risk factors for heart disease and stroke, such as high blood pressure, high cholesterol, and low levels of the vitamin folate, may predispose people to AD. Evidence for physical, mental, and social activities as protective factors against AD is also increasing.

## What Are the Symptoms of AD?

AD begins slowly. At first, the only symptom may be mild forgetfulness. In this stage, people may have trouble remembering recent events, activities, or the names of familiar people or things. They may not be able to solve simple math problems. Such difficulties may be a bother, but usually they are not serious enough to cause alarm.

However, as the disease goes on, symptoms are more easily noticed and become serious enough to cause people with AD or their family members to seek medical help. For example, people in the middle stages of AD may forget how to do simple tasks, like brushing their teeth or combing their hair. They can no longer think clearly. They begin to have problems speaking, understanding, reading, or writing. Later on, people with AD may become anxious or aggressive, or wander away from home. Eventually, patients need total care.

## How Is AD Diagnosed?

An early, accurate diagnosis of AD helps patients and their families plan for the future. It gives them time to discuss care while the patient can still take part in making decisions. Early diagnosis will also offer the best chance to treat the symptoms of the disease.

Today, the only definite way to diagnose AD is to find out whether there are plaques and tangles in brain tissue. To look at brain tissue, however, doctors must wait until they do an autopsy, which is an examination of the body done after a person dies. Therefore, doctors can only make a diagnosis of "possible" or "probable" AD while the person is still alive.

At specialized centers, doctors can diagnose AD correctly up to 90 percent of the time. Doctors use several tools to diagnose "probable" AD, including:

• questions about the person's general health, past medical problems, and the history of any difficulties the person has carrying out daily activities,

• tests of memory, problem solving, attention, counting, and language,

• medical tests—such as tests of blood, urine, or spinal fluid, and

• brain scans.

Some of these test results help the doctor find other possible causes of the person's symptoms. For example, thyroid problems, drug reactions, depression, brain tumors, and blood vessel disease in the brain can cause AD-like symptoms. Some of these other conditions can be treated successfully.

Recently, scientists have focused on a type of memory change called mild cognitive impairment (MCI), which is different from both AD and normal age-related memory change. People with MCI have ongoing memory problems, but they do not have other losses like confusion, attention problems, and difficulty with language. Scientists funded by the NIA are studying information collected from the Memory Impairment Study to learn whether early diagnosis and treatment of MCI might prevent or slow further memory loss, including the development of AD.

Scientists are finding that damage to parts of the brain involved in memory, such as the hippocampus, can sometimes be seen on brain scans before symptoms of the disease occur. The NIA will be funding the AD Neuroimaging Initiative, a study that will find out whether brain scans can diagnose AD early. These brain scans and other potential "biomarkers" have the potential for speeding the testing of drugs for MCI and AD.

## How Is AD Treated?

AD is a slow disease, starting with mild memory problems and ending with severe brain damage. The course the disease takes and how fast changes occur vary from person to person. On average, AD patients live from 8 to 10 years after they are diagnosed, though the disease can last for as many as 20 years.

No treatment can stop AD. However, for some people in the early and middle stages of the disease, the drugs tacrine (Cognex), donepezil (Aricept), rivastigmine (Exelon), or galantamine (Reminyl) may help prevent some symptoms from becoming worse for a limited time. Another drug, memantine (Namenda), has been approved for treatment of moderate to severe AD. Also, some medicines may help control behavioral symptoms of AD such as sleeplessness, agitation, wandering, anxiety, and depression. Treating these symptoms often makes patients more comfortable and makes their care easier for caregivers.

Developing new treatments for AD is an active area of research. Scientists are testing a number of drugs to see if they prevent AD, slow the disease, or help reduce symptoms.

There is evidence that inflammation in the brain may contribute to AD damage. Some scientists believe that drugs such as nonsteroidal anti-inflammatory drugs (NSAIDs) might help slow the progression of AD, although recent studies of two of these drugs, rofecoxib (Vioxx) and naproxen (Aleve), have shown that they did not delay the progression of AD in people who already have the disease. Now, scientists are studying the NSAIDs celecoxib (Celebrex) and naproxen to find out if they can slow the onset of the disease.

Research has shown that vitamin E slows the progress of some consequences of AD by about 7 months. Scientists now are studying vitamin E to learn whether it can prevent or delay AD in patients with MCI.

Recent research suggests that ginkgo biloba may be of some help in treating AD symptoms. There is no evidence that ginkgo will cure or prevent AD. Scientists now are trying to find out whether ginkgo biloba can delay or prevent dementia in older people.

Some studies have suggested that estrogen used by women to treat the symptoms of menopause also protects the brain. Experts also wondered whether using estrogen could reduce the risk of AD or slow the disease. One study showed that estrogen does not slow the progression of already diagnosed AD. Now scientists have found that women over the age of 65 who use estrogen with a progestin are at greater risk of dementia, including AD, and that older women using only estrogen could also increase their chance of developing dementia.

But, more research is needed to find out if estrogen may play any other role. For example, scientists now are trying to find out whether estrogen can prevent development of AD in women with a family history of the disease. They also would like to know whether starting estrogen therapy around the time of menopause, rather than at age 65 or older, will protect memory or prevent AD.

## Testing Treatments

Researchers undertake clinical trials to learn whether treatments which appear promising in observational and animal studies actually are safe and effective in people. Some ideas which seem promising turn out to have little or no benefit when they are carefully studied in a clinical trial.

People with AD and those with MCI who want to help scientists test possible treatments may be able to take part in clinical trials. Healthy people also can help scientists learn more about the brain and AD. The NIA maintains the AD Clinical Trials Database, which lists AD clinical trials sponsored by the Federal government and private companies. To find out more about these studies, contact the NIA's Alzheimer's Disease Education and Referral (ADEAR) Center at 1-800-438-4380, or visit the ADEAR Center website at www.alzheimers.org. You also can sign up for e-mail alerts on new clinical trials that have been added to the database.

Many of these studies are being done at NIA-supported Alzheimer's Disease Centers located throughout the United States. These centers carry out a wide range of research, including studies of the causes, diagnosis, treatment, and management of AD. To get a list of these centers, contact the ADEAR Center.

## Is There Help for Caregivers?

Most often, spouses or other family members provide the day-to-day care for people with AD. As the disease gets worse, people often need more and more care. This can be hard for caregivers and can affect their physical and mental health, family life, job, and finances.

The Alzheimer's Association has chapters nationwide that provide educational programs and support groups for caregivers and family members of people with AD. . . .

## Research

Scientists have come a long way in their understanding of AD. Findings from years of research have begun to clarify differences between normal age-related memory changes, MCI, and AD. Scientists also have made great progress in defining the changes that take place in the AD brain, which allows them to pinpoint possible targets for treatment. These advances are the foundation for the National Institutes of Health (NIH) Alzheimer's Disease Prevention Initiative, which is designed to:

- understand why AD occurs and who is at greatest risk of developing it;
- improve the accuracy of diagnosis and the ability to identify those at risk;
- discover, develop, and test new treatments;
- discover treatments for behavioral problems in patients with AD.

# THE EARLY SYMPTOMS OF ALZHEIMER'S DISEASE

Daniel Kuhn

Daniel Kuhn is the educational director at the Mather Institute on Aging in Evanston, Illinois. He is involved in many studies of the psychosocial aspects of Alzheimer's disease, including one that seeks to measure the quality of life in persons with dementia in various settings. Kuhn has also worked as a licensed clinical social worker in Chicago and served as educational director at the Rush Alzheimer's Disease Center, which is also in Chicago. In the following extract from his book *Alzheimer's Early Stages*, he gives a detailed description of the early symptoms of the disease. According to Kuhn, the general public's perception of Alzheimer's is of the disease's later stages when patients may be fairly helpless and require constant care. He emphasizes that Alzheimer's progresses slowly. At the onset of the disease, people suffer from mild forgetfulness that they are able to hide from their family and friends, sometimes for years. Eventually, however, mental deterioration worsens until patients are no longer able to care for themselves.

Forgetfulness may be sporadic and seem insignificant in early stages of AD [Alzheimer's disease], but it becomes more persistent over time. It may take months or years before you, as a close relative or friend of someone experiencing gradual memory loss, begin to notice any pattern. A particularly troubling incident or a series of minor incidents may trigger an appointment for a medical evaluation. Although persistent memory impairment is the key feature of AD, subtle changes in one or more brain functions such as language, orientation, perception, and judgment may also be evident in the early stages. In this [selection], I describe how the disease may develop in the everyday lives of people with AD.

The early stages of AD usually involve difficulty remembering recent episodes—such as forgetting an encounter with someone or losing or misplacing something. These instances gradually begin to disrupt one's customary lifestyle. The person with early-stage AD may require regular reminders about tasks such as keeping appointments, cooking meals, or paying bills. At the same time, people with early-stage AD appear to think and behave normally much of the time, an appearance that is deceptive, since the progressive microscopic damage to their brains is creating a host of practical difficulties. There may be valiant efforts to hide or compensate for such difficulties, but eventually, others close to the situation sense that something is not quite right. As the disease slowly advances, the need for help becomes more apparent. Therefore it is important to understand the usual signs and symptoms of the disease, as well as many unusual features that may be manifested.

## What Is Recent Memory?

The type of memory affected by AD is generally called "recent memory." A person whose recent memory is impaired typically forgets events that took place within the past hour, day, or week. Entire episodes or fragments of an episode cannot be recalled because new learning does not occur or is disrupted. Recent memory is quite different from remote memory, which involves events, places, or people from the distant past and often remains intact in the early stages of the disease. For example, a person with AD may not be able to recall what she had for breakfast today but may well recall the details of a high school prom some sixty years earlier. The ability to perform personal-care tasks such as dressing and bathing usually remains intact too.

Physicians have made numerous attempts to categorize the different stages of AD, but these classifications have fallen short for one simple reason: There is great variability among affected people in how the disease is first manifested and progresses over time, although impairment of recent memory is the common feature.

## Beginning Signs

What are commonly referred to as the early signs of AD do not actually mark the beginning of the disease but are the first *observable* and persistent signs. Recent research studies have shown that changes in the brain probably occur for years before manifesting as symptoms. Most family members of a person with AD are able to recall unusual incidents that occurred months or years before a loved one was diagnosed. At the time they may have dismissed these signs as nothing more than eccentric behavior or as a normal part of the aging process. Only when a pattern emerges over time are these strange incidents put into the proper perspective. . . .

Since we have no single objective test for diagnosing AD, it is possible for even keen observers to fail to detect the disease in its early stages. The decline in memory often associated with aging confuses the situation. For example, allowances are made for an eighty-year-old person who is a bit forgetful because of the common belief that some degree of memory loss is to be expected at that advanced age. But if the same level of memory loss were observed in a fifty-year-old person, there would be cause for alarm. In other words, societal expectations often come into play in distinguishing between normal and abnormal forgetfulness. . . .

Many people with AD are able to continue compensating for their symptoms, keeping them hidden from others, even their spouses, for months or years. They may deliberately avoid embarrassing situations that challenge their faulty memory. They may quietly retire from their jobs, for instance, after realizing that work demands are becoming too challenging. Once they retire, others may not readily notice their deficits because they no longer have the intellectual demands of a job. At home, they may gradually turn over certain responsibilities to others, such as balancing a checkbook, shopping for food, or preparing income taxes. They may avoid new and unfamiliar places and people, and rely on stock phrases and old memories in conversations instead of revealing their inability to keep track of new details. These are not usually deliberate attempts to cover up, but unconscious efforts to adapt to changes in memory and thinking. Often their spouses and others close to the situation unwittingly adapt to these changes and slowly assume a more active role in the relationship.

## When Symptoms Become Noticeable

Loved ones usually notice the problem once the affected person becomes taxed beyond his or her mental abilities. While daily routines may not reveal much, stressful episodes may bring symptoms of the disease into the open. For example, the drastic change in lifestyle required as a result of a spouse's death is enough to uncover symptoms. In addition to the loss, the spouse can no longer help in taking care of the details of everyday life. In one case, a son describes how he first became aware that there was a serious problem with his mother after his father's sudden death: "I knew [M]om was slipping a bit, but Dad rarely complained. He gradually took over most of the household tasks. After he died, Mom seemed really confused. She not only missed him on an emotional level but on a very practical level too. I had no idea of how forgetful she was until he was gone."

Any significant change in the routine of an affected person may be sufficient to bring out the symptoms of AD. For example, when a person with AD goes on vacation, he or she may experience confusion and may even get lost. One woman traced her first awareness of her husband's AD to their trip to Europe:

First, he did not participate as usual in the planning of the vacation. He seemed anxious while packing his bags. He had trouble remembering the location of hotels as well as our itinerary. He seemed really out of sorts at times but then he would seem okay at other times. He was fine when we got back home, but later I began to notice little things that made me suspicious all over again.

## An Emerging Pattern

Abilities to store, prioritize, and recall new information are brain functions that slowly break down with the onset of AD. At first, family members usually write off these memory lapses as absent-mindedness or a lack of attention. Forgetfulness may be easily overlooked as part of the human experience. After all, there are so many minute details to remember that the brain naturally filters out trivia. However, these incidents eventually become part of a disturbing pattern, indicating AD.

In the early stages, the affected person may be able to remember certain trivial details while forgetting matters of great importance, or vice-versa. Loved ones may rationalize these memory lapses as random blips when, in fact, they may be the initial signs of the disease. In some cases, the person with AD is the first to notice the problem and to complain about changes in memory and thinking.

Forgetfulness in the early stages of AD may take a variety of forms. At first, it is mild and erratic. Those affected forget things more often than they did in the past. They may forget appointments, parts of conversations, or even entire conversations. Even when reminded, they may forget again just minutes later. They may even forget that they have forgotten! Or they may repeat the same statements or questions over and over. Their attempts to compensate by writing out reminders or by having others repeat instructions to them eventually prove inadequate as the problem worsens. They may forget about appointments. They may forget to pay bills or they may pay the same ones more than once. They may forget that they have food cooking on the stove and end up with burned meals. Learning and remembering new information becomes a real problem.

The person with AD typically has good and bad days or good and bad moments within a given day. He or she may remember some things and forget others within the same hour. Ann Davidson writes in her memoir about her husband with AD:

> Julian can't remember that his underpants are in the dresser, yet he usually remembers to come home on time. He doesn't know the location of the wall plugs when he tries to vacuum, yet he knows how to go alone to the library. He's capable in some areas, impaired in others. His abilities fluctuate day-to-day, maddeningly inconsistent. . . .

Family members are usually puzzled by the difficulties that they notice in their loved one for some time before they realize that a disease may be in progress. Most people do not act on their feeling that something may be wrong, or they deny the severity of the problem. Waiting two or three years before seeking out a medical explanation is common. Physicians, in turn, often do not detect the problem during a cursory examination or brief conversation. Consequently, most persons with early symptoms of AD do not receive a thorough assessment and diagnosis. . . .

In addition to persistent loss of recent memory, one or more common symptoms of AD will sometimes be present in the early stages. These include occasional or regular difficulties with reasoning, orientation, language, concentration, spatial relations, and judgment. The appearance of such symptoms over time varies from person to person but all of them usually become prominent as the disease advances. At first, however, these difficulties tend to be mild in nature.

## Difficulty with Reasoning

Reasoning, or the ability to think logically, is often the second area that is affected by AD. This impairment typically affects the person's ability to understand or solve practical problems. Like other symptoms in the early stages of AD, this symptom comes and goes. The affected person may become disconcerted if faced with a task involving a series of steps, such as handling money, doing calculations, cooking a meal, driving a car, or using household appliances and tools. Gloria explained that her husband had always been handy around the house but was stumped one day when faced with a relatively simple task:

> The first time I really began to notice there was a problem was one day when he tried to install a screen in the door. He stood there with the screen in his hand, looking at the frame and said to me, "I can't figure out how to do this." Then I began to reflect on other things that hadn't seemed right. I recalled that months earlier he had also said it was getting hard to balance the checkbook and had asked me to figure it out. He had always done the bills. These difficulties he was having were inconsistent, so I think we had been easing into things. When he said, "I can't do this" or "I can't figure that out," I realized that I wasn't just imagining things.

## Disorientation

Confusion about time and space is fairly common in the early stages. The person with AD may get mixed up about directions and become lost or may not know the current day, month, or even year. Bill recounted the first sign of changes in his wife's ability to navigate their community:

> I noticed it in her driving at first. She had lived in our town all her life and always knew how to get around the area. One

day she had to go to the bank and then to the insurance office. However, she had to come home after going to the bank because she didn't know how to get to the insurance company. She was also unable to keep track of her purse and was misplacing things. Her missing purse had become kind of a joke for the past four years. I think I just kind of grew accustomed to it, not necessarily thinking that it was Alzheimer's.

Letty Tennis writes in a newsletter about her warped sense of time:

> Time means nothing to me. I rarely know the day of the week or the date. This bothers me a lot, but we have worked it out. George just says, "You have an hour before we go, so start getting ready." Since time is not there for me, I nap in my chair sometimes and when I awake, I panic because I can't understand why I'm alone in the house—even though it's a work day for George. I'll dash around the house looking for George, or I'd have this awful feeling that I'm baby-sitting and can't find the children.

In the early stages of AD, affected people don't have as much difficulty with the *mechanics* of speech as they do with the *rules* of speech that make verbal communication effective. They might have trouble finding the right words or remembering names. Their ability to process information may be slowed, resulting in long pauses or lapses in concentration during conversation. The overall richness of their vocabulary may diminish and so may the ability to articulate thoughts and feelings and to comprehend the speech of others. . . .

The first changes Winnie noticed in her husband were in his language ability:

> It was not so much his memory as his speech. Some of his sentences would be backwards. He would mix up the sequence of the words. I was getting frustrated and so I made an appointment with a neurologist, thinking that perhaps he had a mini-stroke or something. He was examined, but all the tests were normal at first. Another year passed before his doctor agreed that his memory problem had progressed and his coordination had started to diminish a bit. Only then did the doctor say he had Alzheimer's.

## Difficulty with Concentration, Spatial Relations, and Judgment

A person's ability to concentrate or to pay attention may diminish in the early stages of AD. This difficulty may manifest itself in reading with little or no comprehension or in being unable to follow a conversation. An individual may respond slower than usual to everyday situations. Richard noted that his wife often commented on her growing difficulty with conversations: "Sometimes during conversation, she would be talking and then there would be a lapse in conversation and she would say, 'Oops! The train left the track! What were we talking about?'"

The human eye depends on the brain to organize and interpret what is being seen. Judging distances and recognizing familiar people or objects are sometimes difficult for a person in the early stages of AD. In effect, the brain distorts visual images. This phenomenon, known as "agnosia," is an unusual first symptom in the early stages of AD. The following stories by two spouses highlight how a difficulty with spatial relations heralds additional symptoms.

Frances recalled that her husband was the first to notice changes occurring in his depth perception:

> He said he was tripping on stairs because he was having difficulty determining the space between them. It was as if the stairs were running together. He also complained that words appeared jumbled on printed pages. He would see things from afar and grossly misjudge their appearance. Of course, we thought it was his eyes at first, but the ophthalmologist said his eyes were fine. A short time later the memory problem emerged. Again, he was the first one to notice this too!

Don described his wife's early symptoms as difficulty with judging distances while driving, with other symptoms following:

> About three years ago she was involved in a car accident on a road that was wide enough for eight trucks to go through, and yet she hit a parked car. I sensed that something wasn't normal when she had a couple more fender benders. After that, there wasn't really anything until last spring when I noticed she was forgetful, leaving purses, not taking messages, and she was not as neat with her appearance. Nothing drastic, but something was different. Also, people who didn't see her frequently would ask me what was wrong with her. They said she wasn't the same person—she wasn't outgoing or fluid with her speech and movement and thinking. I think it was the fact that other people were telling me that my wife had changed that made me aware of the fact that she was having these problems.

Making sound decisions depends on memory to an extent, but also requires logic and reasoning. Distortions in the thought process may lead a person with AD to make inappropriate decisions, even though she may believe she has made a correct choice. For example, one man in the early stages of AD impulsively bought an expensive new car, even though he could not afford it. In another case, a woman gave away most of her life savings to an unscrupulous neighbor. Another woman with AD turned up the thermostat in her home to eighty-five degrees, and the intense heat nearly killed her.

## Personality Changes

In addition to the intellectual impairments described above, certain other symptoms may be present from time to time or regularly. These include a range of personality changes, delusions, and changes in sexuality, physical coordination, and the sense of smell. Again, not everyone with the disease has these symptoms. They tend to appear occasionally in the early stages and become more common in the later stages of the disease, but the frequency and severity of these symptoms vary from person to person.

Personality changes are seldom dramatic in the early stages of AD. However, the affected person may not seem like his or her "old self" in some ways. The most notable change is usually diminished drive or lack of initiative. People who are normally active may become passive, assertive people may start deferring to others. People in the early stages of AD may show a lack of interest in people and activities that they previously enjoyed, such as family gatherings, social events, and hobbies. These changes in mood and behavior are often misinterpreted as a symptom of depression. Although symptoms of AD and depression can occur together, generally speaking a loss of initiative may be due solely to AD and may be unresponsive to treatment with antidepressants. Luke recounted the change in his wife after they had relocated to another state: "She had a complete change in her personality once we got there. She normally was outgoing and curious but she became a recluse. She wouldn't go anywhere without me. After a while, the confusion and memory problems set in."

Some people with AD may become self-centered and ignore the feelings of others. Such insensitivity may be offensive to others unless it is correctly interpreted as a sign of the disease. Judy initially worried that her marriage was falling apart because of the change in her husband's personality:

> He no longer seemed interested in me, which was quite out of character for him. He became increasingly self-absorbed, to the point that I thought he didn't care about me, or anybody else for that matter. I was beginning to believe that our marriage was on the rocks for the first time in forty-nine years.

Some people with AD may become less inhibited in their speech and behavior. Someone who may have been calm and patient in the past may now seem short-tempered. Likewise, someone known to be passive and quiet may become opinionated and outspoken. Impulses previously held in check may no longer be fully controlled. For example, a daughter complained that her mother, who had AD, had always been "prim and proper" but had developed a pattern of expressing herself in an offensive way: "My mother never used foul language in the past, but now she is doing it freely with no hint of embarrassment. She can swear a blue streak, which can be very embarrassing. It's almost comical at times."

Sometimes people with AD may express a surprising degree of irritability or even outright aggression toward others, especially loved ones. Such disturbing behaviors typically stem from their feeling fatigued, overwhelmed, or frustrated. It is important for you to remember that verbal and physical outbursts are symptoms of the disease, and should not be interpreted as personal attacks. There is almost always an underlying cause that triggers these unpleasant occurrences. To the person with AD, hostile remarks and acts may be means of self-defense in response to situations that they perceive as threatening or to the confusion wrought by the disease. It may take some detective work . . . to figure out what triggers the antisocial behavior and how to minimize it or prevent it from happening again.

## Delusional Thinking

Delusions refer to false, fixed beliefs. In AD, they usually take the form of allegations, such as of infidelity, financial exploitation, and similar personal offenses, against others close to the affected person. Delusional thinking is actually rare in the early stages of AD, and it is typically coupled with the loss of recent memory. Delusions may appear so irrational and out of character that they stir family members to seek a medical explanation. Peter noted that his wife became convinced that he was having an extramarital affair, in spite of all evidence to the contrary:

> She began to accuse me of infidelity—for the first time in fifty-two years of marriage! She claimed that whenever I left her alone I was seeing another woman. It was completely absurd, but she became wildly jealous and suspicious. All my efforts to reassure did not help. Only later did I understand this behavior as a symptom of her disease.

In another case, Joan's mother-in-law accused her of stealing some of her clothing. "It was preposterous to imagine that I would be interested in her clothes. She apparently misplaced some of her things and decided to blame me for some strange reason. She was convinced that I was at fault. Her continuing accusations really strained our relationship for a while."

## Behavioral Changes

Healthy sexuality depends on a variety of complex physical and psychological factors related to the brain, and there is some evidence that sexual dysfunction may be common in the early stages of AD. Diminished sex drive is probably the biggest issue. Men may have difficulty attaining or maintaining an erection, while women may experience lack of vaginal lubrication. Whether these problems are related to disruption in brain pathways affecting sexual arousal or are a psychological reaction to other changes in the brain due to AD is not yet known. Maria described her husband's sexual difficulties: "He wanted to have sex, but he was unable to sustain an erection. After a while he gave up trying and I thought it was perhaps my fault. That was about the same time I first noticed his memory problem."

Sexual interest may actually sometimes increase in the early stages of the disease. Josephine explained the change in her husband's sex drive:

> We had always enjoyed a close, loving relationship, but he became even more amorous after he suddenly retired. I later found out that his retirement was linked to his declining job performance. Shortly thereafter, I began to notice his problems with memory and thinking. Although his brain was failing, his sexual appetite was growing!

Because of embarrassment, many affected people unfortunately never address these sexual changes. Marriages may suffer over this sensitive matter, and spouses may retreat from each other or get into conflict. Partners of those with AD should recognize that changes in sexual functioning are not necessarily a sign of problems in the relationship. Rather, a diminished or heightened sex drive should be seen within the context of other symptoms associated with AD and should be discussed openly.

## Diminished Coordination

Although mobility and other physical functions are typically unchanged in the early stages, sometimes a person with AD may walk cautiously or slower than usual, or have difficulty with getting up from a chair or out of bed. Most people with AD have minor difficulty with complex and fine motor functions involving eye-hand coordination and rapid hand movements, which may be manifested in illegible handwriting or trouble using utensils or tools. This motor impairment may also get in the way of driving a car safely. How AD damages certain nerves and muscles while leaving most of the affected person's physical abilities intact is not yet fully understood.

## Diminished or Lost Sense of Smell

There is also strong evidence that people with AD tend to lose their sense of smell. This sensory deficit by itself is not indicative of the disease, since it can be caused by many other factors. Nevertheless, a lost sense of smell should be seen as another potential symptom of AD.

The early stages AD are characterized primarily by loss of recent memory but may be accompanied by other symptoms. Loved ones may notice these subtle changes, but they are easy to miss. As the disease slowly advances, seemingly disconnected incidents of forgetfulness and other warning signs of brain dysfunction begin to form a troubling picture. You and others who are close to the person with AD should acknowledge disturbing changes and recognize that a medical problem is probably unfolding. A proper diagnosis, treatment, and planning are indicated for the sake of all concerned.

# DIAGNOSING ALZHEIMER'S DISEASE

Alzheimer's Association

The next selection is an extract from a pamphlet created by the Alzheimer's Association to help people who may be suffering from Alzheimer's to obtain the most accurate diagnosis possible and to understand that diagnosis. The diagnosis process is divided into six parts: a determination of a person's medical history, an evaluation of their mental status, a physical examination, a neurological exam, laboratory tests, and a psychiatric evaluation. The selection also suggests ways for people to prepare for the diagnostic tests of a family member they suspect has Alzheimer's. The association recommends that family members keep notes on any changes in the person's abilities, behavior, and personality, and provides a list of questions they are likely to be asked during the initial appointment. The Alzheimer's Association is a national voluntary organization that provides information and services to people affected by Alzheimer's. Its stated mission is "to eliminate Alzheimer's disease through the advancement of research and to enhance care and support of individuals, their families and caregivers."

Memory loss and changes in mood and behavior are some signs that you or a family member may have Alzheimer's disease. If you have noticed these signs, it is important to receive a diagnosis for the following reasons:

- Many things can cause dementia, a decline in intellectual ability severe enough to interfere with a person's daily routine. Dementias related to depression, drug interaction and thyroid problems may be reversible if detected early.
- Other causes of dementia include strokes, Huntington's disease, Parkinson's disease and Pick's disease. Alzheimer's disease is the most common cause of dementia. It is important to identify the actual cause in order for the individual to receive the proper care.
- The individual who may have Alzheimer's disease may be able to

maximize the quality of his or her life by receiving an early diagnosis. It may also resolve the anxiety of wondering "What is wrong with me?"

• An early diagnosis allows more time to plan for the future. Decisions regarding care, living arrangements, financial and legal issues, and other important issues can be addressed.

• Alzheimer's disease is known to strike persons in their 40s and 50s. This "early onset" form of Alzheimer's disease presents unique planning issues for the individual and family.

• A diagnosis enables you to establish a family medical history with Alzheimer's disease. . . .

## The Diagnostic Process

There is no one diagnostic test that can detect if a person has Alzheimer's disease. The diagnosis is made by reviewing a detailed history on the person and the results of several tests, including a complete physical and neurological examination, a psychiatric assessment and laboratory tests. Once these tests are completed, a diagnosis of "probable" Alzheimer's disease can be made by process of elimination. However, physicians can be 80 to 90 percent certain their diagnosis is accurate. The process may be handled by a family physician or may involve a diagnostic team of medical professionals, including the primary physician, neurologist (a physician specializing in the nervous system), psychiatrist, psychologist and nurses.

The diagnostic process generally takes more than one day and is usually performed on an outpatient basis. It may involve going to several different locations or even to a specialized Alzheimer diagnostic center. The local chapter of the Alzheimer's Association can refer you to physicians and/or diagnostic centers in your area.

## The Six Steps to Diagnosis

The diagnostic process involves the following:

*1. Determination of Medical History.* The person being tested and family members will be interviewed both individually and together to gather background information on the person's daily functioning, current mental and physical conditions, and family medical history.

*2. Mental Status Evaluation.* During the mental status evaluation, the person's sense of time and place, and ability to remember, understand, talk and do simple calculations will be assessed. The person may be asked questions such as: "What year is it?" "What day of the week is it?" "Who is the current president?" The person will also be asked to complete mental exercises, such as spelling a word backwards, writing a sentence, or copying a design.

When reviewing the test results, the physician will consider the individual's overall performance in relation to his or her educational background and occupation.

*3. Physical Examination.* During the physical exam, the physician will evaluate the person's nutritional status and check blood pressure and pulse. The physician will also search for the presence of cardiac, respiratory, liver, kidney and thyroid diseases, and atherosclerosis (hardening of the arteries). Some of these conditions can cause dementia-like symptoms.

*4. Neurological Exam.* A physician, usually a neurologist, will closely evaluate the person's nervous system for problems that may signal brain disorders other than Alzheimer's disease. The physician will search for evidence of previous strokes, Parkinson's disease, hydrocephalus (fluid accumulation in the brain), a brain tumor, and other illnesses that impair memory and/or thinking. The physician will learn about the health of the brain by testing coordination, muscle tone and strength, eye movement, speech and sensation. For example, the physician will test reflexes by tapping the knee, check the person's ability to sense feeling on their hands and feet, and listen for slurred speech.

*5. Laboratory Tests.* A variety of laboratory tests will be ordered by the physician to help diagnose Alzheimer's disease by ruling out other disorders. A complete blood count and blood chemistry will be ordered to detect anemia, infection, diabetes, and kidney and liver disorders. Levels of vitamin B 12 and folic acid (a vitamin produced by the body) are measured, as low levels can be associated with dementia. Since very high or low amounts of the thyroid hormone can cause confusion or dementia, levels of the thyroid hormone are measured through a blood test.

The physician may also order an EEG (electroencephalogram) to detect abnormal brain wave activity. This test can detect conditions such as epilepsy, which can sometimes cause prolonged mild seizures that leave a person in a confused state.

A CT (computerized tomography) scan, which takes X-ray images of the brain, is also frequently used. The brain is scanned for evidence of tumors, strokes, blood clots and hydrocephalus. MRI (magnetic resonance imaging) is another brain-imaging technique sometimes used. More experimental tests may also be recommended but are not necessary for the diagnosis. These include PET (positron emission tomography), which shows how different areas of the brain respond when the person is asked to perform different activities, such as reading, listening to music, or talking; and SPECT (single proton emission computed tomography), which shows how blood is circulating to the brain.

*6. Psychiatric, Psychological and Other Evaluations.* A psychiatric evaluation can rule out the presence of other illnesses, such as depression, which can result in memory loss similar to dementia of the Alzheimer type. Neuropsychological testing may also be done to test memory, reasoning, writing, vision-motor coordination and ability to express ideas. These tests may take several hours, and may involve interviews with a psychologist, as well as written tests. These tests provide more in-depth information than the mental status evaluation.

Nurses, and occupational, rehabilitation or physical therapists may be called upon to look for problems with memory, reasoning, language and judgment affecting the person's daily functioning.

## Understanding the Diagnosis

Once testing is completed, the diagnosing physician or other members of the diagnostic team will review the results of the examinations, laboratory tests and other consultations to arrive at a diagnosis. If all test results appear to be consistent with Alzheimer's disease, the clinical diagnosis will be "probable Alzheimer's disease" or "dementia of the Alzheimer type." If the symptoms are not typical, but no other cause is found, the diagnosis will be "possible Alzheimer's disease."

Although researchers have made enormous progress in diagnostic testing, the only way to prove Alzheimer's disease is through an autopsy.

If a cause of dementia other than Alzheimer's disease is diagnosed, call the Alzheimer's Association to request a free informational brochure about related causes of dementia.

## The Family's Role in Diagnosis

While some people with Alzheimer's disease may initiate their own diagnosis and care, for most, it will be up to another family member to alert the physician. Here are some tips that will help you get someone to the physician for an initial evaluation:

• Schedule the appointment for the person.

• Help with transportation to the appointment.

• Read this [article] as a family to gain a better understanding of what to expect during the diagnostic process.

• Contact your local chapter of the Alzheimer's Association if you have any concerns or questions.

• Offer to accompany the person during the testing process if he or she is still uneasy about investigating possible Alzheimer's disease.

On the day of the appointment, bring along items such as glasses, hearing aids, devices that help the person walk, a list of medications the person is taking, and other personal items that might help during diagnostic testing. Be sure the physician has all medical records, insurance and social security information.

## Preparing for Diagnostic Tests

Once the initial appointment has been made to evaluate a person, the diagnostic team will need certain information to make an accurate diagnosis. [Following are] questions that you may be asked by the diagnostic team, as well as questions that you may want to ask regarding the diagnostic process. It may be helpful to start writing down events that occur, and any changes in the person's abilities, behavior and personality that cause you to suspect Alzheimer's disease.

*Questions You May Be Asked:*
- What symptoms have you noticed?
  - Difficulty performing simple tasks?
  - Recent memory loss that affects job skills?
  - Poor or decreased judgement?
  - Others?
- When did the symptoms first appear?
- How have the symptoms changed over time?
- Does the person suffer from other medical conditions?
- Is the person taking any medications?
- Have other family members been diagnosed with Alzheimer's disease?

*Questions to Ask Before Diagnostic Testing:*
- Which tests will be performed?
- Will any of the tests involve pain or discomfort for the person?
- How long will the tests take?
- How long will it take to learn the results of the tests?

*Questions to Ask If the Diagnosis Is Probable Alzheimer's Disease:*
- What does the diagnosis mean?
- What symptoms can be anticipated next?
- How will they change over time?
- What level of care will be required now and in the future?
- What medical treatment is available?
- What are the risks and effectiveness?
- What changes should be made in the home to make it safer?
- What resources and support services are available in our community?
- Are experimental drug trials available?

Alzheimer's disease is not currently preventable, but science and medicine continue to make promising advances. Obtaining an early and accurate diagnosis is an important strategy in helping to improve the quality of life for persons with dementia and their families.

# CHAPTER 2

# POSSIBLE CAUSES OF ALZHEIMER'S DISEASE

# THE SEARCH FOR THE GENETIC CAUSES OF ALZHEIMER'S

Rudolph E. Tanzi and Ann B. Parson

In their book *Decoding Darkness: The Search for the Genetic Causes of Alzheimer's Disease*, Rudolph E. Tanzi and Ann B. Parson describe their long search for the genetic causes of Alzheimer's. In this excerpt they describe the strong evidence they found for a link between the A2M (alpha-2-macroglobulin) gene and Alzheimer's disease. They also explain why they believe that learning more about A-beta will unlock further secrets about Alzheimer's disease's origins and how it functions in the body. A-beta is the name of the protein that makes up the amyloid plaques that are often found in the brains of Alzheimer's patients. Rudolph E. Tanzi is an associate geneticist at Massachusetts General Hospital and a professor at Harvard Medical School. Ann B. Parson is a science journalist and the author of *The Proteus Effect: Stem Cells and Their Promise for Medicine*.

As this book travels to press, biology's Big Bend has been rounded. Scientists from Celera Genomics and the federally funded Human Genome Project have jointly announced, well ahead of time, that they've all but decoded humankind's DNA and its letters of life. It was only in 1995 that science read the first genome of an independent organism—a bacterium named *Hemophilus influenzae* (1,743 genes). Yeast followed in 1996, the first cracked code of an organism with a cell nucleus and therefore kin to all plants and animals (6,000 genes). Two years later, scientists unveiled the entire sequence of the first multicellular organism—C. *elegans*, the minute dirt worm (19,099 genes).

And now *Homo sapiens*. At last human genetics will have its own Table of Elements for reference. But it's early in the day, with lots more to do. We still need to pick out and make plain the vast numbers of genes within the genome's sequence. And left to identify are the vast numbers of proteins made by genes, their various functions in the body, and, if flawed, the consequences. This could take the better part of the century, although genetic knowledge of other organisms should help out. For instance, each gene—hence protein—in yeast exists in like form in humans.

Let's just hope that as we lean on kindred genomes for insight into our own, we'll gain greater respect for all life. We and the mouse, after all, have genomes that are roughly 97 percent similar. And let's hope that this broader sensibility will guide us in how we will apply our mountain of new knowledge. As [head of the author's lab at Mass General] Jim Gusella frequently notes, "All knowledge is good; the only concern is how it's used."

## Genetic Links to Alzheimer's

As for those human genes connected to Alzheimer's, new reports support our Mass General team's belief that the A2M [alpha-2-macroglobulin] gene is a late-onset culprit, a run of case-control studies having failed to consistently find such evidence. Three teams adopted the novel family-based technique that led us to A2M and confirmed a correlation between A2M variants and an increased disease risk. Three other groups have tied A2M to increased brain amyloid [plaque found in the brains of Alzheimer's patients]. At Mass General, meanwhile, the large NIMH [National Institute of Mental Health] DNA screening is revealing several hits for other late-onset genes, with one very strong candidate on chromosome 10. A published report from Ellen Wijsman's lab at the University of Washington suggests that, altogether, five to six major aberrant genes may be involved in late Alzheimer's.

Despite sharper statistical tools, geneticists' biggest problem continues to be securing total proof of a late-onset gene's unruliness, and how it joins with other internal and external factors to bring on the disease. With over a dozen Alzheimer candidates being scrutinized by various labs, and undoubtedly numerous others to be hauled into view, it could take many years to achieve a full accounting. Similar to the genes already cornered, many of us expect that those left to identify somehow inveigle A-beta's toxic buildup.

## Evidence from Related Disorders

In mid-1999, Blas Frangione's NYU lab isolated yet another dementia-associated amyloid protein, one that in my view provides an intriguing parallel to what might be happening in Alzheimer's disease. In some ways, Familial British Dementia is markedly different from Alzheimer's; it's rare and, like several other amyloidoses, mostly confined to the brain's blood vessels. Patients' gray matter contains tangles and some dense amyloid plaques, but many more diffuse plaques. A chief similarity, however, is that a gene mutation (on chromosome 13) translates into high levels of an insoluble fibril that free-floats between gray-matter neurons. Distinct from, yet comparable to, Alzheimer's A-beta, this fibril just might be driving neuronal death. It would appear that all it takes is copious, accumulating amyloid fibrils of any type in memory regions to trigger inflammation, tangles, neuronal loss, and dementia. As to why, in this rare disease, dense plaques don't overrun gray matter, the nature of its fibril may not allow for their formation.

Making for rapt discussion among neuroscientists is the fairly new realization of just how many brain disorders follow the same course—from gene mutation to a mucked-up, misfolded protein that fibrilizes and forms rock-hard aggregates the body can't get rid of. Along with Alzheimer's, examples of other maladies that give rise to brain deposits of one form or another—in the following cases, usually inside the cell—include Parkinson's disease, which promotes tiny clusters called Lewy bodies; the prion diseases and their bunching prion rods; Lou Gehrig's disease and its multiple inclusions; and Huntington's and other neuro-disorders that spring from overly repetitious DNA and load brain cells with insoluble particles.

"It's very exciting to see these commonalities emerging," notes Anne Young, Mass General's chief of Neurology Service. "In none of these disorders have protein fragments or their aggregates been proven to be the sole source of the disease, but in several cases the fragments are very likely toxic. Many of these diseases develop slowly, so there's all the more hope of interfering with their aggregating proteins." As for Alzheimer's, it's lately been noticed that aside from its profuse extracellular A-beta, A-beta can accumulate *inside* neurons. Although cell amounts are minuscule, intensive research has begun to determine whether they are harmful.

## The Importance of A-beta

Several fresh findings indeed square with the conviction that amyloid fibrils are a driving component of Alzheimer's pathological stream.

To mention but a few, Mike Mullan and coworkers have seen strong evidence in mice that the A-beta peptide activates the immune system's microglia, which, as we've described, may contribute to the demise of neurons. The University of South Florida team further has shown that if you keep microglia from reacting to A-beta's presence, you might reduce neuronal loss, which suggests yet another drug target to pursue.

For all those who thought "hogwash" when Dennis Selkoe's lab proposed that Alzheimer's presenilin 1 protein might itself be the gamma-secretase, one of A-beta's liberating proteases, lately both a Merck team and Selkoe's lab independently lassoed more direct evidence. That PS1 may be the gamma-secretase demands more proof, but if it stands up, just as drugmakers are doing with the recently nabbed beta-secretase, compounds might be made to fly in the face of presenilin with the intent of reducing A-beta fibrils.

Two studies lend further credibility to the idea that accumulating

A-beta in the brain is Alzheimer's weapon of mass destruction. Bruce Yankner's group at Children's Hospital discovered that injected A-beta has a toxic effect on the brains of older monkeys, but not younger primates or mice. This would seem to indicate the extent to which aging acts as a susceptibility factor in Alzheimer's, and that A-beta's toxicity is specific not only to older brains but to species with more highly developed brains. It's tempting to think this might explain why transgenic mouse models overloaded with A-beta fail to exhibit substantial neuronal loss.

Finally, a study by Joseph Buxbaum's team at Mount Sinai and collaborators at Rockefeller University and Albert Einstein has shown a strong correlation between total elevated A-beta and the progression of dementia. It cannot be concluded that A-beta is forcing the insidious onset of dementia. Yet if there were any doubts regarding a correlation between mounting brain A-beta and mental decline, this study should do away with them.

## Possible Drug Therapies

On the drug front, one of the most hopeful recent findings was made by Karen Duff's NYU group. After demonstrating that a high-fat diet increases A-beta's production in male transgenic mice, the researchers went on to dose the mice with a cholesterol-lowering drug and, so promisingly, saw A-beta levels diminish. Using the same type drug, Konrad Beyreuther's lab at the University of Heidelberg observed a reduction of normal A-beta levels in guinea pigs. Should too much A-beta in the brain be Alzheimer's fatal flaw, both experiments point to a treatment that's readily available. Precisely how cholesterol-lowering drugs work against A-beta remains a mystery.

In January 2000, my colleague Ashley Bush e-mailed glad tidings from Australia. "Holy Fenoki! Could it be???" his message exclaimed. In a second set of tests, our company's metal-extracting compound had reduced total fibrillar A-beta in the brains of aged twenty-one-month-old transgenic mice by about 50 percent. (In transgenic mice of this age, it's usually hard to find a part of the cortex that isn't overwhelmed with plaques.) Not expecting anywhere near this magnitude of effect, I was totally surprised. Our previous positive results in younger mice just might have been a fluke. The company is currently proceeding to phase one of clinical trials to assess the drug's safety. Once we see safety, we greatly look forward to phase two and testing the compound's efficacy in patients.

With plentiful signs indicating that useful Alzheimer drugs may be on the way, increased attention is being focused on developing sound diagnostic tools. Good diagnostics are critical if, for the sake of preventative measures, we hope to catch sight of Alzheimer's earliest inner changes years ahead of its obvious symptoms. As [researcher] Zaven Khachaturian has pointed out, while Alzheimer's mostly appears later in life, it is actually a younger person's disease, since its abnormalities fester years before they become manifest. The most beneficial diagnostics will be those that can pick out the disease's genetic faults in a person's genome; or detect its earliest biochemical alterations in the blood and/or spinal fluid; or spot structural changes in the brain.

## Diagnostic Tools

In the early-onset category, predictive blood tests currently exist for some of the discovered early-onset mutations. Commercially available, they are performed within the framework of a larger neurological examination in many academic medical settings. Each of these tests requires genetic and psychological counseling as well as legal safeguards that ensure confidentiality on the part of the center administering the exam. Some at-risk individuals who have a parent with early Alzheimer's, and who might be experiencing memory loss themselves, want to be tested, for it can help them and their families make important decisions about the future. But since no effective drugs are yet available, most of those at risk very understandably would rather not know.

In the late-onset category, blood tests exist for the APOE [at risk, early onset] variant. But . . . while APOE-4 can boost the risk for Alzheimer's, it does not guarantee the disease. Therefore, in most situations APOE testing is not recommended.

Aside from genetic testing, several other diagnostic approaches are being developed. One of the most promising is MRI—magnetic resonance imaging. When used to scan the brains of people who are either genetically prone to or already displaying dementia, MRI can monitor whether regions central to memory—the entorhinal cortex or hippocampus, in particular—are undergoing shrinkage indicative of Alzheimer's. Another use of MRI currently under development will allow doctors to view plaques and tangles directly. Even if these lesions are late-stage phenomena, mounting numbers might provide an early warning. When effective drugs arrive, MRI also might serve to monitor a drug's ability to slow plaque-tangle formation and the brain's volume loss.

In April 2000, a study by Marilyn Albert's Mass General crew, in which my lab collaborated, showed that MRI, when trained on changes in the entorhinal cortex of patients with mild forms of forgetfulness, can indicate how soon a patient will convert to full-blown Alzheimer's. Researchers had guessed the entorhinal cortex degenerated early on. Now to actually *see* direct evidence, to be able to actually watch the disease progress in a living person, is quite amazing. It gives us a way of tracking the rate and severity of the disease's progression; of knowing, for the sake of applying drugs, who will get the disease sooner than later.

There continue to be high hopes that someday, by measuring a specific altered protein in the body, doctors will have a marker that easily reveals whether someone harbors a susceptibility to Alzheimer's. To that end, investigators continue to gauge whether a blood or spinal fluid test can determine elevated A-beta 42 or abnormal tau.

## A Vision for the Future

In the future, the ultimate indispensable diagnostic might be a person's genotypic profile. Someone's entire genome might be put on a biochip that is outfitted with all the mutations and polymorphisms known to cause Alzheimer's. Their DNA would either bind or not bind to those danger points. A computer scan of the chip would handily reveal any DNA defects, doing away with the time-consuming methods that currently allow us to assess a person's gene alleles. The resulting profile might relate other valuable pieces of information, such as a person's overall risk for Alzheimer's (depending on which aberrations are present); the time window of onset; and which treatments will be most effective and which could carry adverse side effects.

A futuristic vision for conquering Alzheimer's wraps around the powerful combination of genetic screening—always accompanied by counseling and stringent safeguards—and preventative drugs optimized for a person's genome. A foundation is being laid right now for such an eventuality. The year might be 2010 or later. A person with a family history of Alzheimer's, or perhaps no family history, decides to be assessed for his or her predisposition to Alzheimer's. Family history is reviewed; a genotypic profile is obtained; levels of A-beta, tau, and perhaps other relevant proteins are measured. A baseline measurement of certain brain regions is retrieved through MRI. Should this workup sound an alarm, were just one magic bullet available—a vaccine, for instance—that would obviously be the therapy of choice. But more likely a range of treatments would be required and dispensed according to a person's age, genetic profile, and disease stage. Should fibrillar A-beta turn out to be Alzheimer's demon, a daily A-beta cocktail might be prescribed that thwarts A-beta in a number of ways—by inhibiting the secretases' activity, by blocking A-beta aggregation, and by promoting its clearance. Other drugs could assuage the menacing biochemical features in the disease's cascade or promote neuronal regeneration. Short of curing Alzheimer's, the goal would be to make it a manageable chronic condition.

Currently, there's a growing awareness that the last thing we want to do, in terms of treatment, is to prolong late-stage disease, suspending a patient in a terrible state of nonidentity. An important clinical decision will be at what stage it may be too late to treat someone. Equally important will be the decision of how early to begin treatment. Since it appears that the disease's molecular wrongs commence relatively early in life, there's reason to think that intervention might start at a fairly early age. This seems a small price to pay were it possible to silence Alzheimer's.

By mid-century, new estimates warn, the world may contain 45 million Alzheimer patients—three times as many as there are now. Bring on effective drugs, and a good many of those individuals just might be able to experience their golden years with a clear mind and sound recollection.

# Phosphate Fertilizers and Aluminum May Contribute to Alzheimer's

Lynn Landes

In the following article Lynn Landes questions why more Americans suffer from Alzheimer's than any other population in the world. She hypothesizes that the phosphate fertilizers used in American agriculture in combination with the aluminum that is found in drinking water, foods, and many consumer products might be causing many Americans to develop Alzheimer's disease. She accuses federal agencies of not seriously investigating possible environmental causes of Alzheimer's. Lynn Landes is a freelance journalist who writes about the environment, health, and politics.

Americans are losing their minds to Alzheimer's disease. It's an epidemic. And it's not typical of what's going on in the rest of the world.

The World Health Organization (WHO) estimates that there are 18 million people with Alzheimer's. Over 4.5 million Americans have the disease. We account for 25 percent of all Alzheimer's cases, even though we represent only 4.6 percent of the world's population. Europe is experiencing half our rate of disease. For Americans over eighty-five years of age, 50 percent are thought to have Alzheimer's.

The question is, "Why?"

Alzheimer's was first discovered in 1906. It is not a part of normal aging, says the National Institutes of Health (NIH). The NIH contends that the cause of Alzheimer's is "not known." They say, "Prior theories regarding the accumulation of aluminum, lead, mercury, and other substances in the brain have been disproved."

Don't believe that. Federal agencies have a talent for not finding environmental causes for many diseases. They live by the motto, "Do not seek and thou shall not find." Genetic triggers and lifestyle choices get the research dollars for pretty obvious reasons—their findings don't hurt polluters' profits.

The world's scientists and government researchers have not taken aluminum off the scientific table as a causal factor in Alzheimer's. Re-

Lynn Landes, "Alzheimer's in America: The Aluminum-Phosphate Fertilizer Connection" *Food and Water Journal*, October 31, 2000, p. 14. Copyright © 2000 by Wild Matters. Reproduced by permission of the author.

search scientists with the International Aluminum Network report, "Aluminum has been implicated . . . as a potential factor or cofactor in the Alzheimer's syndrome, as well as in the etiopathogenesis of other neurodegenerative diseases, Parkinsonism, Amyotrophic Lateral Sclerosis and other diseases." That's a mouthful, but you get the picture.

Initially, it was thought that aluminum might be the sole cause of Alzheimer's. Persons with Alzheimer's have been found to experience increased absorption of aluminum in the brain, as well as exhibiting densities of senile plaques and neurofibrillary tangles. However, there are reports that suggest plaques and tangles do not always signify Alzheimer's, and vice versa.

Further clouding the issue are patients on kidney dialysis machines. They are unable to excrete aluminum, plus they may also be treated with medicines that include aluminum. However, reports say that dialysis patients don't develop Alzheimer's, although they can develop dialysis dementia if the equipment doesn't filter out aluminum. And therein lies a clue.

## Clues About Aluminum

The process of kidney dialysis requires very purified, nonfluoridated water. What does this mean? Perhaps fluoride is aluminum's partner-in-crime.

In 1998 Julie Varner and two colleagues published research on the effects of aluminum-fluoride and sodium-fluoride on the nervous system of rats. They concluded, "Chronic administration of aluminum-fluoride and sodium-fluoride in the drinking water of rats resulted in distinct morphological alterations of the brain, including the effects on neurons and cerebrovasculature." In layman's terms, it looked like fluoride and aluminum could cause Alzheimer's.

That was not a definitive study, but they may have been onto something. Aluminum is in our drinking water, foods, and many consumer products. Adding fluoride to drinking water in the United States started in the 1950s. America's drinking water is now over 60 percent fluoridated. Fluoride appears in many processed foods and beverages made with fluoridated water. Keep in mind, Europe has half our rate of Alzheimer's. Europeans don't fluoridate their water supplies, but they do use fluoride supplements and dental products. Is there a connection?

There are other intriguing issues. Why do people with thyroid disease have an increased risk for Alzheimer's? In the United States, thyroid disease has reached even greater epidemic levels than Alzheimer's, with as many as 20 million American victims. Besides problems with iodine intake, a common cause of thyroid disease is radiation.

There are also striking similarities between Alzheimer's, Creutzfeldt-Jacob-Disease (CJD), and mad cow disease. Mad cow has been linked to livestock feed and fertilizer.

So, what do radiation, livestock feed, fluoride, and fertilizer have in common, which may have led to the emergence of the Alzheimer's epidemic? The phosphate fertilizer industry.

## The Fertilizer Industry

"Fertilizer use was not a common practice in the United States until after 1870, when phosphate and lime were applied to crops like cotton and tobacco. By the end of World War II, an era of intensive agriculture began . . . ," says Cargill Fertilizer [Corporation]. "Of the phosphate produced in Florida, about 95 percent is used in agriculture (90 percent goes into fertilizer and 5 percent into livestock feed supplements)." The remaining 5 percent is used in a variety of foods and beverages, plus personal care, consumer, and industrial products.

George Glasser writes in the *Earth Island Journal*, "Radium wastes from filtration systems at phosphate fertilizer facilities are among the most radioactive types of naturally occurring radioactive material wastes. . . . Uranium and all of its decay-rate products are found in phosphate rock, fluorosilicic acid (fluoride) and phosphate fertilizer."

The Florida Institute of Phosphate Research says, "Removal of uranium as a product is no longer profitable and all of the extraction facilities have been dismantled. The uranium that remains in the phosphoric acid and fertilizer products is at a low enough level that it is safe for use." That's not reassuring. Chronic exposure to low levels of contamination can be as dangerous, or more so, than chronic high levels of exposure or acute occurrences.

Of particular interest is calcium silicate, another by-product of the phosphate fertilizer industry. One of its uses is as an anticaking agent in iodized table salt. Is calcium silicate also radioactive? Would that have a significant impact on the thyroid? Given the relationship between Alzheimer's and thyroid disease, Alzheimer's may be destined to increase exponentially.

The phosphate fertilizer industry seems to be the common thread in Alzheimer's—and maybe also in thyroid and mad cow–type diseases. Aluminum by itself may not cause Alzheimer's, but in combination with the radioactive products of the phosphate fertilizer industry, it could be wreaking havoc on our health.

Whatever the cause, we deserve real answers to the Alzheimer's epidemic, not the red herrings of research on genetics and lifestyle. The number of American victims is totally out of proportion to the incidence of Alzheimer's worldwide. Something truly has gone terribly wrong.

# Repetitive Head Injury May Lead to Alzheimer's Disease

*AIDS Weekly*

The following selection describes experimental evidence found by researchers at the University of Pennsylvania School of Medicine indicating that there is a direct link between repetitive head injury and Alzheimer's disease. The researchers conducted their study using a breed of mice developed specifically for this research. The transgenic mice possess the human gene that produces amyloid beta (Ab) protein. Deposits of this protein in the brain are believed by many researchers to contribute to the development of Alzheimer's. In studying the mice, the researchers at the University of Pennsylvania found that repetitive head trauma led to an increase in the deposit of Ab protein and an acceleration in the development of the symptoms of Alzheimer's. The study is important not only because it points to a possible cause of the deposit but because the special mice developed for it may also be used to test treatments for Alzheimer's.

Researchers at the University of Pennsylvania School of Medicine have found direct evidence that mild, repetitive head injuries can lead to Alzheimer disease.

Their evidence suggests that brain trauma accelerates Alzheimer by increasing free radical damage and the formation of plaque-like deposits of amyloid beta (Ab) proteins. Perhaps just as important, the special breed of mice developed for the study could serve as a model in screening drugs to treat Alzheimer and traumatic brain injuries.

"This is the first experimental evidence linking head injuries to Alzheimer disease by showing how repetitive concussions can speed up the progress of the disease," said Kunihiro Uryu, PhD, a senior research investigator at Penn's Center for Neurodegenerative Disease Research (CNDR). "It also shows the tremendous utility of the transgenic mice and the trauma model we have developed for Alzheimer research."

In recent years, researchers have made remarkable progress in un-

*AIDS Weekly*, "Alzheimer's Disease: Repetitive Head Injuries Can Lead to Senility," February 4, 2002. Copyright © 2002 by NewsRX. Reproduced by permission.

covering the genetic basis of inherited Alzheimer disease. They do not, however, know much about the causes of the sporadic, or noninherited, forms of the disease, despite the fact that almost 90% of all Alzheimer cases can be termed sporadic.

While there are a few documented genetic risk factors that predispose a person to Alzheimer, one very robust environmental factor, head trauma, has been identified. Although recurrent head trauma is thought to cause Punch Drunk Syndrome (dementia pugilistica) in boxers, researchers had been unable to prove a mechanistic link between head injury and Alzheimer.

## Better Experiments

Until now, however, researchers have lacked a good animal model for studying the development of Alzheimer disease. Their findings are published in the January 15, 2002, issue of the *Journal of Neuroscience*.

The transgenic mice used in the CNDR contain the human gene that produces the Ab protein. With the aid of techniques developed at the Penn Head Injury Center, Uryu and his colleagues were able to study how just mild repetitive head injuries could influence the progress of Alzheimer disease. Even without head trauma, these mice would eventually develop Ab plaques later in life. With the trauma, they produce symptoms of Alzheimer disease at a remarkably increased rate.

"Here, we can clearly see a direct cause and effect relationship between repetitive concussions and Alzheimer," said John Q. Trojanowski, MD, PhD, codirector of the CNDR and professor in the Department of Pathology and Laboratory Medicine. "Using the head trauma model in these mice represents a step forward in our ability to understand the basic molecular mechanisms behind Alzheimer disease. More importantly, we believe this model system can be used to screen for new medications in the search for a cure."

While there are a number of medications that treat the symptoms of Alzheimer, there are no medications, as yet, that address the root of the disease.

Over the course of the study, mice were sedated and given mild repetitive concussions. In the ensuing weeks, Uryu and his colleagues monitored their behavior and brain pathology.

In addition to looking for deposits of Ab, they also monitored amounts of a molecule called isoprostane. Last year [2001], Penn researchers discovered that urine isoprostane levels serve as an indicator of the sort of free radical damage found in Alzheimer disease.

"Two days after the injuries, and again at 9 and 16 weeks, we measured amyloid deposits and levels of isoprostanes and amyloid beta proteins," said Uryu, "At each point, we saw a dramatic increase of indicators for Alzheimer disease in the mice that received repetitive head traumas."

According to their findings, repetitive—but not single—mild, traumatic brain injuries increased Ab deposition as well as levels of Ab and isoprostanes in the transgenic mice. The repetitive injuries induced cognitive impairments in the mice, but did not interfere with their motor functions and dexterity.

"Alzheimer disease has a very real and understandable molecular basis and it will be curable," said Trojanowski. "Developing a working animal model of how head trauma augments Alzheimer pathology, as we have in our studies here, is just one more step in reaching the inevitable treatment."

# CHAPTER 3

# RESEARCH ON THE PREVENTION AND CURE OF ALZHEIMER'S

# Dietary Fat, Vitamins, Estrogen, and the Prevention of Alzheimer's

Gabrielle Strobel

This article by Gabrielle Strobel reviews recent findings on the effects of fat consumption, vitamins C and E, and estrogen replacement therapy on the development of Alzheimer's disease. Despite many studies, researchers have been unable to prove that there is a link between total fat intake and the development of Alzheimer's. In addition, recent research calls into question previous assumptions that vitamins E and C reduce the risk of Alzheimer's. Strobel also describes a study that suggests that estrogen therapy does not improve cognition or mood in women with mild or moderate Alzheimer's. Furthermore, she notes that additional research suggests that higher estrogen levels may actually decrease memory skills. Gabrielle Strobel is managing editor for the Alzheimer's Research Forum, a Web site that publishes research about Alzheimer's.

A foursome of papers in the February 17 [2003] Archives of Neurology continues the shifting debates about three epidemiological questions in Alzheimer's research.

Let's consider first the one bit of positive results. Martha Clare Morris and colleagues at Rush-Presbyterian/St. Luke's Medical Center in Chicago report their analysis of the Chicago Health and Aging Project, an observational community study to identify risk factors for Alzheimer's. They found that a diet high in saturated and trans-unsaturated fats (partially hydrogenated fats found in many processed foods) correlated with an increased risk of developing AD [Alzheimer's disease] whereas a diet low in those fats but high in vegetable fat, as well as mono- and polyunsaturated fat, correlated with a decreased risk in a cohort of 815 white and African American people 65 years and older. The researchers followed the study participants for a mean of 3.9 years and analyzed the contents of different types of fat in a food frequency questionnaire that most of the participants had filled out once before the study began.

The Chicago study used a questionnaire similar to those developed by Walter Willet and colleagues at the Harvard School of Public Health and used in the Nurses and Physicians Health Studies conducted by these investigators. Morris's results also roughly follow that study insofar as it found a similar pattern of fat types associated with changes in AD risk as the Harvard group had previously found for coronary heart disease.

Mono- and polyunsaturated fats tend to reduce LDL cholesterol, while saturated fat and trans-unsaturated fats tend to increase it. Consumption of vegetable fat was protective, but intake of dietary cholesterol did not correlate with AD risk. That last finding may still fit into the developing hypothesis on cholesterol and AD, since saturated fat intake determines serum cholesterol levels more strongly than does dietary cholesterol, the authors note.

More broadly, findings on the fat connection are far from unanimous. Morris and colleagues quote a prior study from the Rotterdam group, drawn on a larger cohort than the Chicago study, which supported a link between dietary fats and AD risk. Yet, since the Morris paper was accepted for publication last August [2002], the Rotterdam researchers have reported in their own follow-up study that they could not confirm this original link. On the other hand, a study by Jose Luchsinger, Richard Mayeux, and colleagues did find that a diet high in calories and fat might increase one's AD risk, but that study did not analyze the contribution to risk of individual types of fat, but instead focused more on the selective vulnerability to dietary fat of people with the ApoE4 allele. [The ApoE4 allele has been identified as a genetic risk factor for late-onset Alzheimer's.] Morris and colleagues did not find this link between total fat intake and AD risk, leaving this topic wide open for further investigation.

## The Case for Vitamins Weakens

So much for the good news. The bad news concerns vitamins and estrogen. Jose Luchsinger and colleagues at Columbia University in New York poured some cold water on the widely held notion that the antioxidant vitamins C and E can reduce AD risk by counteracting the contribution of oxidative stress to the underlying neurodegeneration in AD. Only last June [2002], both Martha Morris's group and Monique Breteler's group from Erasmus University in Rotterdam had found support for vitamin E, though only Breteler's study found support also for vitamin C. Molecular and cell biology work also supports this idea, and many people already take these vitamins. Yet, when Luchsinger, Mayeux, and others analyzed 980 elderly participants of the Washington-Heights Inwood Columbia Aging Project, they did not see an association with decreased AD risk for either of these vitamins, regardless of whether the vitamins were taken as dietary supplement or in foods. None of the three recent studies confirmed a role for carotene.

Why the discrepant results? All these studies share the limitation that food frequency questionnaires, though validated previously and widely used in epidemiology, are relatively crude instruments. They depend on people's recollection at a given point in time of foods and supplements they take over long periods of time; they don't measure accurately what a person actually consumes every day, or how that changes. One of the differences between the New York and the Rotterdam cohorts was that people in the New York study were older, implying that the Rotterdam study may have been able to capture a preventive effect that the New York study didn't. Furthermore, Luchsinger et al. caution that the numerous discrepancies among these three studies raise the question whether some of the results may be due to chance. They also point to past experience with cardiovascular disease, where observational studies had implicated vitamins C and E, but subsequent clinical trials did not confirm the benefit. Experiences with NSAID [nonsteroidal anti-inflammatory drugs] treatment so far have been similar. Eventually, primary prevention trials must settle the question.

## Estrogen as a Treatment

The other set of disappointing news deals a blow to earlier, hopeful results on estrogen replacement therapy to improve cognition and mood in women with AD. Abundant epidemiological and preclinical work over the past decade had suggested a protective effect for estrogen. Then, in the year 2000, three clinical trials failed to substantiate this claim, instead showing that estrogen therapy did not increase the performance of a total of 210 treated women on global cognitive or functional scales. And yet, two small pilot trials led by Sanjay Asthana, at the University of Washington in Tacoma, did find tantalizing improvements in attention and verbal memory in six of 12 women treated with a transdermal estrogen patch.

In the present study, Leon Thal and Mike Grundman of the University of California, San Diego, with colleagues there and elsewhere, report that they further analyzed their original trial data of 120 women with mild to moderate AD who received Premarin for one year. This multicenter ADCS [Alzheimer's Disease Cooperative Study consortium] trial had been published previously. In light of the pilot trials' success, however, Thal et al. wondered if perhaps some women in the ADCS trial who had higher estradiol levels [estradiol is the most potent of the estrogen steroids] in their blood had indeed responded, but their improvements had gone unnoticed in the overall results. Maybe it was just a question of dose?

To answer this question, the researchers correlated these women's change in plasma estradiol levels with their change in seven neuropsychological measures, including specific tests of memory, attention, and language. They found that baseline estradiol levels were not linked to test performance. Estradiol levels increased to means of 20 (in women on low-dose Premarin) and 40 (on high-dose Premarin) picograms/milliliters, but these elevated estradiol levels still did not correlate with test performance, or cause any significant improvements. The only exception, a negative link to one test, disappeared when the researchers removed three outliers[1] with extremely high estradiol levels from the analysis.

What to make of this? Most cognitively healthy women who currently receive HRT [hormone replacement therapy] across the country and abroad have levels of supplementation around 6 pg/mL, the authors write. The mean estradiol concentrations achieved in this ACDS trial are higher than that, but well below the 75 to 130 pg/mL achieved in the Asthana et al. trials. The estradiol concentration range in treated ACDS patients did reach up to peak levels of 140 mg/mL, and even these did not predict improved test scores. "We conclude that the results obtained by Asthana et al. are most likely secondary to the use of the small sample sized and the presence of a few outliers," the authors write. While this study thus cools hope for estrogen as a treatment for women with mild to moderate Alzheimer's, it does not address the separate question of estrogen as a preventive measure in younger women.

## Estrogen and Memory

Finally, another downer for the estrogen hypothesis comes in a study led by Monique Breteler and colleagues in Rotterdam and elsewhere. These scientists asked whether people with higher estrogen levels had larger hippocampal volume and better memory than those with low estrogen levels. This notion had grown, in part, out of findings that estrogen receptors are especially densely strewn throughout the hippocampus, and out of animal studies on the benefits of estrogen on synapse formation and survival of hippocampal neurons. Perhaps ERT [estrogen replacement therapy] prevents atrophy of the hippocampus, one of the brain areas affected early on in AD? Indeed, William Jagust of the University of California, Davis, had reported at the 2001 Society for Neuroscience Conference in San Diego that the hippocampus was larger in postmenopausal women who were taking estrogen replacement therapy than in postmenopausal women not taking hormones or a group of elderly men. This study has not yet appeared in print but the abstract, No. 550.2, is accessible at http://sfn.ScholarOne.com/itin2001/.

First author Tom den Heijer and colleagues approached the question of estrogen, hippocampal size, and memory performance by analyzing subjects in the Rotterdam Scan Study, an imaging spinoff of the

---

1. Outliers are a kind of extreme value in statistics.

ongoing 13 year-old population-based Rotterdam Study. The Rotterdam Scan Study took MRI brain scans, including a hippocampal volume measurement, of 563 elderly people without dementia. Participants underwent a Mini-Mental State examination and a delayed
recall test of verbal memory, and donated blood for estradiol serum
measurement. The present analysis included 412 study subjects with
data on total estradiol, for 311 of whom the scientists also had data
on bioavailable and free estradiol levels.

Contrary to their expectations, the scientists found that women
with higher estradiol levels had smaller hippocampal volumes and
poorer memory performance than did women with lower estradiol
levels, while in men there was no link between estradiol levels and
hippocampal size, and only a trend for poorer memory with higher
estradiol levels.

The authors point out that while the community-based nature and
large size of MRI sample size are a strength of this study, it also had
limitations. Incomplete data on free and bioavailable estradiol reduced the sample size, and the blood samples were drawn several
years before the MRI, though the influence of that delay in normal
people without dementia is unclear. The authors conclude a brief review of the literature on estrogen, cognition, and AD by writing: "The
biological plausibility of the estrogen hypothesis in dementia is its
strongest plea, whereas studies in humans are far from conclusive."

# EXERCISE MAY HELP PREVENT ALZHEIMER'S

Majid Fotuhi

In this excerpt from his book *The Memory Cure*, Majid Fotuhi describes studies suggesting that exercise leads to better memory and may decrease the likelihood of developing Alzheimer's. One group of researchers found that exercising increases levels of a protein called brain-derived neurotrophic factor, which improves the health of brain neurons. Exercise has also been shown to increase the levels of another beneficial protein, nerve growth factor. A Canadian study found that the more people exercise, the less likely they are to develop Alzheimer's. Although no one has determined exactly how many hours of weekly exercise will protect people from memory loss, it is clear that being physically active improves people's mental health. Majid Fotuhi is a faculty member in neurology at Harvard Medical School and a neurology consultant at the Alzheimer's Disease Research Center at Johns Hopkins Hospital.

An article in the *New England Journal of Medicine* in March 2002 showed that people who exercise more live longer. Researchers looked at the 6213 men who were referred for an exercise tolerance test. They measured how long each person was capable of running on the treadmill. Over six years, 1256 of these individuals died of various causes. More of these patients were from the group who could not run for a long time. For each extra minute they could run, their risk of dying was 12 percent less.

Hundreds of other studies have established the positive link between exercise capability and better overall health. Regular physical activity improves your blood circulation, heart function, sexual performance, and mood. It also lowers blood pressure, reduces tension, and helps you lose weight. Now researchers are discovering that exercise improves your memory and reduces your risk of dementia later in life.

Richard Camicioli, M.D., from the University of Alberta, and his colleagues at the University of Oregon recently monitored a group of

108 healthy men and women from sixty-eight to one hundred years old, over a six-year period, by obtaining brain MRIs, performing cognitive tests, and measuring how fast they could walk thirty feet.

As expected, they found that those who had shown a smaller hippocampus on their MRI or those who had a great deal of difficulty with their memory at baseline were more likely to develop cognitive decline over the period of the research study. Surprisingly, however, they also discovered that those who walked slower at baseline were more prone to memory loss; for every second that they were slower, their risk was 1.14 times higher. Using physical fitness as a prediction for a person's risk of mental decline is a new concept.

In the "Canadian Study of Health and Aging," involving 4615 elderly men and women over the age of sixty-five, Kenneth Rockwood, M.D., and others in several provinces in Canada discovered that people who did more exercise were less likely to develop Alzheimer's disease. They monitored these individuals over five years, from 1991–92 to 1996–97, and noted that 436 of them developed mild cognitive impairment and 285 developed dementia. Those with the highest level of regular physical activity had cut their likelihood of having cognitive impairment or dementia [including Alzheimer's] by half.

In a similar long-term study of 6000 elderly women in California, Kristine Yaffe, M.D., and her colleagues at UCLA found an impressive correlation between more walking and better memory performance. Over six to eight years, these researchers monitored the level of physical activity and memory performance in this group and discovered that the more miles a woman walked on a daily basis, the lower her risk of becoming demented. For each daily extra mile, there was a 13 percent improvement in memory compared to women who walked less.

Jeffrey Kaye, M.D., at Oregon Health & Science University, reported at the American Academy of Neurology meeting in Denver in 2002 that even those in their seventies and eighties lower their risk of developing dementia if they exercise. He and his researchers studied a group of 147 healthy men and women for approximately six years and found that those who exercised vigorously were more likely to ward off dementia.

## How Does Physical Activity Lead to Better Memory?

A few new discoveries are providing exciting clues to answer this question. In an article in the June 2002 issue of *Trends in Neuroscience*, a group of scientists from the University of California reported the possible link between exercise and better memory. They focused their attention on a protein called *brain-derived neurotrophic factor*, or BDNF. This natural protein improves neuronal health and survival. It makes neurons more resistant to injury caused by a stroke and helps with synthesis of new synapses.

The scientists measured the levels of BDNF in the brains of mice who were sedentary, and in the brains of those that had a wheel in their cage and voluntarily exercised for many hours each night. The results were that the more miles the mice ran, the higher the level of BDNF in the hippocampus. Animals unable to make an adequate amount of BDNF had memory problems, which improved once BDNF was injected directly into their brains. In short, BDNF may be one of the key players in mediating the effects of exercise for improved memory. The levels of another protein, called *nerve growth factor*, have also been shown to increase with exercise.

These findings may explain why people who are more physically fit seem to have a better memory and stave off dementia. It encourages people to use exercise not only as a way of living longer, but also to keep the mind sharp during the last decades of their lives. The findings also provide hope for individuals who already have Alzheimer's disease. It may sound like science fiction, but scientists are considering surgically implanting these growth-factor proteins in the brains of patients with Alzheimer's disease to see if they'll get better.

## How Much Exercise Is Enough?

No one has established an exact number of hours of exercise that will protect the brain against memory loss. The data seem to show that the more, the better. In all the published studies, there's a linear relationship between the level of daily activity and the benefits of exercise for improved memory. The current recommendation of the American Heart Association is for people to engage in moderately intense physical activity for at least thirty minutes on most—and preferably all—days of the week. In a recent study of 73,743 women between the ages of fifty and seventy-nine, researchers from Harvard Medical School found that even two and a half hours of brisk walking a week on a regular basis can lower vascular heart disease by 30 percent.

Walking has been shown to lower blood pressure, increase the level of good (HDL) cholesterol, reduce the risk of stroke by half, delay the onset of diabetes in overweight people, reduce the risk of osteoporosis in women by 30 percent, increase gastrointestinal mobility, increase relaxation, reduce stress, and improve memory.

# Intellectual Activity and Positive Emotions May Protect Against Alzheimer's

Michael D. Lemonic and Alice Park

The following article by Michael D. Lemonic and Alice Park describes how David Snowdon, now a scientist at the University of Kentucky, developed a study of the nuns at the convent of the School Sisters of Notre Dame on Good Counsel Hill in Minnesota. He first visited the convent when he was a young assistant professor at the University of Minnesota looking for a research project. He recognized that nuns are ideal candidates for an epidemiological study on aging for two reasons: First, the nuns have almost uniform lifestyles in the convent, which prevents confounding factors from influencing study results; second, upon entering the convent in their early childhood, the nuns submitted pieces of writing containing family and life history information, which offered clues about their odds of developing dementia. Snowdon found that the nuns who submitted more complex writing samples were less likely to develop the outward symptoms of Alzheimer's than were nuns whose writing was more simplistic. He also found that the nuns who expressed more positive emotions in their writing samples were less likely to exhibit symptoms of Alzheimer's. Michael D. Lemonic and Alice Park are reporters for *Time* magazine.

It's the day after Easter, and the first crocus shoots have ventured tentatively above the ground at the convent on Good Counsel Hill. This is Minnesota, however; the temperature is 23°F and the wind chill makes it feel far colder. Yet even though she's wearing only a skirt and sweater, Sister Ada, 91, wants to go outside. She wants to feed the pigs. But the pigs she and the other nuns once cared for have been gone for 30 years. Sister Ada simply can't keep that straight. In recent years, her brain, like a time machine gone awry, has been wrenching her back and forth between the present and the past, depositing her without warning into the days when she taught primary schoolchildren in Minnesota or to the years when she was a college student in St. Paul. Or to the times when she and the sisters had to feed the pigs several times a day.

Like some 4 million Americans, Sister Ada (not her real name) is suffering from Alzheimer's disease; as the years go by, she'll gradually lose her memory, her personality and finally all cognitive function. But advanced age does not automatically lead to senility. Ada's fellow nun, Sister Rosella, 89, continues to be mentally sharp and totally alert, eagerly anticipating the celebration of her 70th anniversary as a sister without the slightest sign of dementia. In a very real sense, this pair of retired schoolteachers haven't finished their teaching careers. Along with hundreds of other nuns in their order, the School Sisters of Notre Dame, they have joined a long-term study of Alzheimer's disease that could teach the rest of us how to escape the worst ravages of this heartbreaking illness.

The groundbreaking research they are helping conduct probably won't lead directly to any new drugs, and it's unlikely to uncover a genetic or biochemical cause of Alzheimer's. Doctors know, however, that preventing disease can be a lot easier and cheaper than trying to cure it. It was by studying the differences between people who get sick and people who don't—the branch of medical science known as epidemiology—that doctors discovered the link between smoking and lung cancer, between cholesterol and heart disease, between salt and high blood pressure. Epidemiology also led to the understanding that cooked tomatoes may help protect against prostate cancer, and that fruits and vegetables tend to stave off cancers of all sorts.

Now it's Alzheimer's turn. Precious little is known about this terrible illness, which threatens to strike some 14 million Americans by 2050. Its precise cause is still largely mysterious, and effective treatments are still years away. But epidemiologists are beginning to get a handle on what kinds of people are most seriously ravaged by Alzheimer's—and, conversely, which people tend to escape relatively unscathed.

Much of this knowledge comes from a single, powerful piece of ongoing research: the aptly named Nun Study, of which Sisters Ada and Rosella are part. Since 1986, University of Kentucky scientist David Snowdon has been studying 678 School Sisters—painstakingly researching their personal and medical histories, testing them for cognitive function and even dissecting their brains after death. Over the years, as he explains in *Aging with Grace*, a moving, intensely personal account of his research that arrives in bookstores this week [May 2001], Snowdon and his colleagues have teased out a series of intriguing—and quite revealing—links between lifestyle and Alzheimer's.

Scientists know that genes can predispose people to Alzheimer's disease. But as described in nearly three dozen scientific papers, Snowdon's study has shown, among other things, that a history of stroke and head trauma can boost your chances of coming down with debilitating symptoms of Alzheimer's later in life; and that a college education and an active intellectual life, on the other hand, may actually protect you from the effects of the disease.

Perhaps the most surprising result of the Nun Study, though, is the discovery that the way we express ourselves in language, even at an early age, can foretell how long we'll live and how vulnerable we'll be to Alzheimer's decades down the line. Indeed, Snowdon's latest finding . . . reinforces that notion. After analyzing short autobiographies of almost 200 nuns, written when they first took holy orders, he found that the sisters who had expressed the most positive emotions in their writing as girls ended up living longest, and that those on the road to Alzheimer's expressed fewer and fewer positive emotions as their mental functions declined.

These findings, like many of Snowdon's earlier conclusions, will undoubtedly spark a lively debate. As laboratory scientists and clinicians are quick to point out, cause and effect are notoriously difficult to tease out of population studies like this one, and exactly what the emotion-Alzheimer's link means has yet to be established. But even hard-nosed lab scientists admit that the Nun Study has helped sharpen the focus of their research. The study has impressed the National Institutes of Health enough that it has provided $5 million in funding over the past decade and a half. "It is," says Dr. Richard Suzman, director of the National Institute on Aging, "a very innovative, pioneering study."

Snowdon wasn't out to change the world when he first began visiting the convent of the School Sisters of Notre Dame on Good Counsel Hill in Mankato, Minn. He wasn't even planning to study Alzheimer's disease. Snowdon was desperately trying to find a research project that would secure his position at the University of Minnesota. He was a young assistant professor of epidemiology at the time—a field he'd been introduced to as a young boy who raised chickens to earn money. "I learned a lot about what it takes to stay healthy from taking care of those chickens," he recalls. "That's what epidemiology is all about—the health of the whole flock."

Chicken studies wouldn't cut it with the Minnesota administration though, so Snowdon was interested when a graduate student, an ex-nun, told him about the aging sisters at her former order, living out their retirement in a convent just two hours away. He was already familiar with the advantages of studying religious groups, whose relatively uniform backgrounds mean fewer variations in lifestyle to confound the data. An order of nuns whose economic status, health care and living conditions were especially uniform would be an excellent starting place for an epidemiological study of the aging process. So he went out for a series of visits. Both Snowdon and the sisters had to overcome inhibitions—theirs at becoming research subjects, his from a Roman Catholic school background that made him uncomfortable asking personal questions of a nun. But they finally agreed that he would quiz them periodically to learn about what factors might be involved in promoting a healthy old age.

At first, the study didn't look as if it would reveal much. For one thing, Snowdon wasn't really sure what aspect of aging to focus on. For another, he had to count on the nuns to recall those aspects of their lives, including the years before entering the order, that had differed—and memory, even among the mentally competent, is notoriously unreliable. But then, after several months, he stumbled on two olive-green metal file cabinets—the personal records of all the young women who had taken their vows at the Mankato convent. "Everything changed when we discovered the archives," says Snowdon.

Because the records were relatively standardized, Snowdon could extend his study of aging far beyond the few years in late life that such studies traditionally cover. Most precious of all were the autobiographies written by each sister on her entry into the order. They were full of basic information about where the sisters were born, who their parents and siblings were, and why each one decided to join the order. With these documents, moreover, Snowdon now had an objective measure of the sisters' cognitive abilities while they were still young and in their prime. An epidemiologist could not have designed a better way to evaluate them across time. "For many years," says the National Institute's Suzman, "we had an inadequate sense of how connected late-life health, function and cognition were to early life. But in the past decade, spurred by the Nun Study, there is a growing appreciation for that connectedness."

The first results, compiled after a year of research, confirmed earlier studies suggesting that people with the most education were most independent and competent later in life (most of the sisters were teachers; many had master's degrees). And breaking with academic tradition—but establishing one of his own—Snowdon first presented his conclusions, not through a journal or a conference but directly to the nuns. Recalls Sister Rita Schwalbe, then one of the convent's administrators: "He threw us a thank-you party, and we thought that was it."

Not even close. Snowdon's study attracted the attention of leading Alzheimer's researchers, who explained to him that the elderly women represented an ideal population for studying this mysterious disease. On average, 10% of people over 65 come down with Alzheimer's, a number that rises to 50% by age 85. Given the aging population of the convent, they knew that a significant proportion of the nuns would have the disease.

The most serious drawback to studying the sisters for Alzheimer's is that there's only one sure way to diagnose it: examine the patient's brain after he or she dies. If he were to proceed, Snowdon would need written permission to perform autopsies, not only on the Mankato nuns but also, to get a large enough sample, on members of the order at six other Notre Dame convents as well. "They really had to trust us," he says. "We could have turned out to be Dr. Frankensteins for all they knew."

So one day in 1990, a nervous Snowdon stood in front of the assembled sisters in Mankato, many of whom he'd got to know as friends, and made his pitch. "We sat in our chairs and held our breath," recalls Sister Rita Schwalbe, who by then had joined Snowdon's research team. "Then one of the sisters piped up, 'He can have my brain, what good is it going to do me when I'm six feet under?' And that broke the ice."

In all, more than 90% of the sisters living in the Mankato convent agreed to donate their brains. After visiting six other convents, Snowdon ended up with a 68% consent rate overall, one of the highest in any tissue-donation study. "I didn't really know what it was going to be about," says Sister Nicolette, an engaging 93-year-old who is the only one of the 16 girls who took their vows in 1925 to both survive and remain mentally intact. "But I thought if science could learn something from this program, then I was glad to be a part of it." In 1991, the first participant, a resident of Good Counsel Hill convent, died, and the Nun Study received its first brain.

Snowdon, who had accepted a position at the University of Kentucky's Sanders-Brown Center on Aging, was working with a team of neurologists and psychologists to devise a battery of tests for assessing the sisters' mental and physical abilities—tests that could later be correlated with the results of brain exams. He joined forces with James Mortimer, an eminent researcher on aging then at the Minneapolis Veterans Administration Medical Center, to study the nuns' youthful autobiographies in more detail, and their relationship led to an interesting discovery: autopsies by other scientists had shown that the physical destruction wrought by Alzheimer's didn't inevitably lead to mental deterioration. The reason, according to one leading theory, was that some folks might have an extra reserve of mental capacity that kept them functioning despite the loss of brain tissue.

So he and Mortimer, along with University of Kansas psychologist Susan Kemper, began analyzing the autobiographies for evidence of such extra capacity. Kemper, an expert on the effects of aging on language usage, had earlier shown that "idea density"—the number of discrete ideas per 10 written words—was a good marker of educational level, vocabulary and general knowledge. Grammatical complexity, meanwhile, was an indicator of how well memory was functioning.

Applying these measures to the sisters' autobiographies, Snowdon and Kemper found to their astonishment that the elderly sisters who showed signs of Alzheimer's had consistently authored essays low in both idea density and grammatical complexity a half-century or more earlier. One of the lowest-scoring samples begins: "My father, Mr. L.M. Hallacher, was born in the city of Ross, County Cork, Ireland, and is now a sheet-metal worker in Eau Claire." By contrast, one of the highest-scoring essays conveys the same type of information but in a dramatically different way: "My father is an all-around man of trades, but his principal occupation is carpentry, which trade he had already begun before his marriage with my mother."

Idea density turns out to be an astonishingly powerful predictor of Alzheimer's disease—at least among the School Sisters of Notre Dame. Snowdon found by reading nuns' early writings, he could predict, with 85% to 90% accuracy, which ones would show the brain damage typical of Alzheimer's disease about 60 years later. "When we first looked at the findings," says Snowdon, "We thought, 'Oh my God, it's in the bag by the time you're in your 20s.'"

But Alzheimer's is not that simple. One especially telling case: Sister Bernadette (not her real name), who had shown no outward signs of Alzheimer's and whose youthful autobiography was rich with ideas and grammatical complexity, turned out at death to be riddled with the plaques and tangles of Alzheimer's. Says Snowdon: "Lesson No. 1 in my epidemiology training is that there are hardly any diseases where one factor alone, even in infectious disease, will always cause illness."

These results posed a chicken-and-egg problem: Did higher brain capacity protect the sisters from developing the symptoms of dementia, or were those with lackluster biographies already suffering very early signs of some brain abnormality that predisposed them to mental decline later? That question remains unanswered—but follow-up studies, to be published next month [June 2001] in the journal *Psychology and Aging*, suggest that exercising what brain capacity you have offers some protection. While all the sisters show age-related decline in mental function, those who had taught for most of their lives showed more moderate declines than those who had spent most of their lives in service-based tasks. And that, says Kemper, supports the commonsense idea that stimulating the brain with continuous intellectual activity keeps neurons healthy and alive. (Of course, notes Snowdon, these activities are not absolute protectors. For some, a genetic predisposition may override even a lifetime of learning and teaching.) . . .

When Snowdon and Kemper first read the sisters' autobiographies in the early 1990s, they noted that the writings differed not just in the density of ideas they contained but also in their emotional content. "At the time," he says, "we saw that idea density was much more related to later cognitive ability. But we also knew that there was something interesting going on with emotions." Studies by other scientists had shown that anger and depression can play a role in heart disease, so the team decided to take another look.

This time they searched for words suggesting positive emotions (such as happiness, love, hope, gratitude and contentment), as well as negative ones (sadness, fear, confusion and shame). Snowdon found that the sisters expressing negative emotions did not live as long as the sisters conveying more positive ones. He has already begun another analysis, comparing the emotional content of the nuns' early autobiographies with the ones they penned in late life, as part of the Nun Study. As mental abilities decline, his preliminary review has found, the expression of positive emotions also drops. While he suspects the whittling away of positive feelings are a consequence of the neurological changes of Alzheimer's, it is still possible that emotional states may play a role in determining cognitive function. To find out, Snowdon will next compare the emotional content of the sisters' writings with their autopsied brains, to see if positive emotions work to keep nerve connections snapping and if negative emotions dampen and eventually extinguish them.

By now, 15 years after he first climbed Good Counsel Hill, Snowdon has identified half a dozen factors that may predict or contribute to Alzheimer's disease. He could sit each sister down right now and tell her what her chances are. But should he? As he has all along, Snowdon will put his dilemma to the sisters themselves: next month he will meet with the Notre Dame leadership to discuss whether to break the news to the high-risk nuns—and, how to answer the inevitable questions about what they might do to prevent or slow down the disease.

"So far," he says, "I have a certain comfort level in making some recommendations because there are other good reasons for preventing strokes, for reading, for taking folic acid. If our findings showed something that had no other known benefit besides preventing Alzheimer's, then we would be on much thinner ice." Even so, it's not clear precisely how much folic acid to take, and Snowdon's team is divided on whether to boost the intake of vitamins C and E beyond the normal recommended doses (Markesbery says yes; Snowdon says not until we know more).

These questions will become more urgent as the population bulge of the baby boom generation reaches the Alzheimer's years—and new research is showing that those years may start earlier than anyone had thought. Just two months ago, scientists suggested that many cases of a condition known as mild cognitive impairment, in which patients in their 40s and 50s exhibit memory and recall problems, are very likely the first step on the way to Alzheimer's disease. If so, then it's important to start slowdown strategies as soon as possible. A cure for Alzheimer's is still the ultimate goal, but, says Snowdon, "until there is a magic bullet that can stop the plaques and tangles from growing, we're going to have to take a multipronged approach that will include things like avoiding head injuries and strokes and adding nutritional supplements like folate and antioxidants."

Meanwhile, the Nun Study will continue. Snowdon and his team are attempting to study the sisters' brains before they die, using MRI scans to track how the brain deteriorates with age and how such changes correlate with those in speech, memory and behavior. And to ensure that the sisters' generous gift to science will continue to educate others, Snowdon is trying to have the brain bank and archive records permanently endowed. That way, future generations will continue to benefit from lessons that women like Sisters Ada, Rosella and Nicolette are teaching all of us about how to age with grace and good health.

# Playing Games, Reading, and Dancing May Reduce the Risk of Alzheimer's

Alzheimer's Association

In 2003 the *New England Journal of Medicine* published the results of a twenty-one-year study of older adults. The study suggests that mental and physical activity help to prevent the development of Alzheimer's disease. The next selection by the Alzheimer's Association describes the study, which involved nearly five hundred adults aged seventy-five and older. The Alzheimer's Association is a national voluntary organization that provides information and services to people affected by Alzheimer's.

Reading books, playing cards and board games, doing crossword puzzles, and dancing may all reduce the risk of developing Alzheimer's and other forms of dementia, according to a report in the June 19 [2003] *New England Journal of Medicine*. This 21-year study of older adults adds to a growing body of evidence on the possibly protective effects of staying mentally active.

"This paper contains the best data that we have so far on this intriguing issue," said Samuel E. Gandy, MD, PhD, vice chair of the Alzheimer's Association Medical and Scientific Advisory Council and professor of neurology, biochemistry, and molecular biology at Thomas Jefferson University. "However, we still need to interpret the results cautiously. There are enormous difficulties involved in comparing the intensity, duration, and challenge of one activity to another. Obtaining definitive data will require devising a novel and truly 'quantifiable' activity that study participants can be randomly assigned to engage in or not."

Gandy and some of his colleagues have speculated that some type of computer-based training or game might meet the need for standardization, but they are unaware of any current attempts to develop one.

This study's somewhat surprising results highlight the difficulties involved in comparing one activity to another. Six activities were clas-

Alzheimer's Association, "Deal Me In: Playing Cards and Board Games, Reading and Dancing May Reduce Dementia Risk," www.alz.org, June 19, 2003. Copyright © 2003 by the Alzheimer's Association, (800) 272-3900. Reproduced by permission.

sified as "mental" and 11 as "physical." Of the mental activities, reading, playing cards or board games, doing crossword puzzles, and playing a musical instrument reduced dementia risk, while writing for pleasure and participating in group discussions did not. Dancing was the only physical activity that lessened dementia risk, although some earlier studies have shown a protective effect associated with staying physically active. The study involved nearly 500 adults ages 75 and older who showed no signs of dementia at the time of enrollment.

The authors suggest three possible explanations for their results:

(1) The effect is real and certain types of mental stimulation somehow help stave off dementia. One possible explanation is "cognitive reserve," the theory that mentally challenging activities stimulate development of richer networks of nerve-cell-to-nerve-cell connections than are found in the brains of people who do not engage in such activities. The richness of these networks provides a "buffer" or "reserve" against the cell degeneration associated with dementia.

(2) The effect is not real, but appears to exist because certain types of mental activity actually represent the influence of other factors that have not yet been identified.

(3) Less frequent participation in mentally challenging activities is actually a subtle symptom of dementia that affects behavior years before the disorder can be diagnosed.

The researchers tried to control for the last possibility by removing from the data analysis anyone who developed dementia within seven years of enrolling in the study. The protective effects of the activities persisted even when data from such individuals were eliminated.

In an editorial accompanying the report, Joseph T. Coyle, MD, from the department of psychiatry at Harvard Medical School, echoes the cautions and the need for definitive data. Yet he concludes, "In the meantime, seniors should be encouraged to read, play board games, and go dancing, because these activities, at the very least, enhance their quality of life, and they just might do more than that."

# CLAIMS THAT ESTROGEN PREVENTS ALZHEIMER'S ARE UNFOUNDED

Barbara Seaman

In this excerpt from her book *The Greatest Experiment Ever Performed on Women: Exploding the Estrogen Myth*, Barbara Seaman argues that despite highly publicized studies that claim that estrogen and other hormone treatments may prevent women from developing Alzheimer's disease, there is no strong evidence that this is true. She explains that one of the reasons for this "estrogen myth" is that the press releases about the studies neglect to mention that the women who feel that their symptoms of memory loss are helped by estrogen therapy are generally those suffering from memory problems associated with menopause rather than from Alzheimer's. She describes many studies that show no link between hormone treatment and Alzheimer's prevention. She also notes that there has been little research into the use of estrogen as a treatment for Alzheimer's. Seaman concludes that more conclusive evidence about the effectiveness of hormone therapy in preventing Alzheimer's must be found before women can be advised to take hormone pills. Barbara Seaman is a cofounder of the National Women's Health Network and the author of several books on women's health. She has also written articles for many periodicals, including the *New York Times, Washington Post*, and *Ladies' Home Journal*.

Many of us can identify with the sixty-six-year-old Harvard professor who forgot her classroom number when ordering a slide projector. She went directly to the office of the university's Alzheimer's specialist and asked, "Am I losing it?" Was she having a senior moment or was it something far worse? Was it Alzheimer's?

Three percent of adults ages sixty-five to seventy-four develop this dread disease, and the percentage rises as age advances. Many of us who have watched a parent or an elderly friend struggle with Alzheimer's debilitating effects live in mortal fear of someday succumbing to the same fate. As baby boomers approach the passage between middle age and senior status, there is overwhelming interest revolving around what can be done to reduce the odds of developing Alzheimer's and upping the chances of preserving memory.

It is very hard to accept the fact that little actually *can* be done, but a desire to be proactive has created a huge market for products claiming to help—products ranging from vitamin supplements to diet and exercise regimens to pharmaceuticals.

Since 1994, with the publication of a paper in the *American Journal of Epidemiology* called "Estrogen Deficiency and the Risk of Alzheimer's Disease in Women," estrogen supplementation and other hormone therapies have been promoted as a way to improve memory and stave off Alzheimer's. This despite the fact that precious little evidence has emerged that estrogen does fight the disease. So how do pharmaceutical companies continue to market the drug as a means of combating AD [Alzheimer's disease]? By conflating normal menopausal memory problems and natural aging-associated cognitive impairment with Alzheimer's; women have been bamboozled into believing that treating the first two means preventing the last.

That we have nothing but the slimmest evidence to support any positive relationship between estrogen and the prevention of Alzheimer's is not for lack of trying. The sheer volume of scientific work that has been done on this topic in the past decade is overwhelming. Even more astounding is how many millions of dollars it has taken us to conclude that there is no good evidence that estrogen either prevents or treats Alzheimer's disease, and that as of yet, the relationship between hormones and AD is not understood. . . .

## Science by Press Release

The prescribing of hormone therapy for Alzheimer's disease exploits this painful situation and is an example of gender-based drug marketing at its most blatant. It relies on the running together of two unrelated memory problems: normal menopausal "mind" lapses—which are often temporary but nonetheless upsetting—and Alzheimer's, as if the first can lead to the second, a claim for which there is no scientific evidence. Promoting estrogen as prevention against Alzheimer's is a classic example of "science by press release," a practice whereby essential information is deliberately omitted. Just as some doctors conceal that the most dramatic changes in bone mass are shown to occur in castrated women, they may also fail to explain that the women who feel sure their brains are benefiting from estrogen are generally those in menopause who have experienced the normal phenomenon of memory problems. As one woman described what she called her brain fog: "I stammered, I stuttered, I misread words. It's as if the coordination between my eyes and the rest of me just didn't connect. I found myself searching for the most basic one- or two-syllable words whereas I previously was extremely articulate. For a smart-ass like myself, this process was terribly frustrating."

Such trouble organizing and expressing ideas can challenge a woman's self-image. A friend explains that "I can look up and down a bookshelf for ages without finding the title I want, and it's right in front of me. I must say, I am profoundly 'hurt' by this. . . . Reading, writing, discussing, finding the perfect word within our elegant language—all these things were my idea of having a good time. Now what? If I lose my health insurance because my brain no longer functions well enough to hold down a job, that will surely shorten my life!"

Many women feel they would do almost anything to avoid or rectify these problems, making it easy for the drug companies to hook them on hormone therapy.

One woman who went on estrogen said that the "deciding factor for me in trying hormone therapy was brain function—I was losing mine! My memory was really, really bad. I spent more time going in circles than I did accomplishing anything. Sometimes I forgot what I was saying in the middle of a sentence and had this crazy inability to understand the spoken word. I was fine with anything in print or on a screen, but things people said to me sometimes sounded like gobbledygook. That was *very* scary."

## Proof Against Estrogen

The belief that hormones can help menopausal women with memory and concentration is not totally unfounded. There have been studies for some years now that suggest a relationship between estrogen and cognitive function. The connection, however, has been largely undefined and overstated. A study published in 2000, dealing with postmenopausal estrogen and progestin use and cognitive change in older Japanese American women, set out to test both the connection between estrogen and cognition and the potential difference that estrogen alone might make as opposed to an estrogen/progestin combination pill. The conclusion: Both estrogen and progestin seemed to have a beneficial effect on cognition. However, the report on the study steered scrupulously clear of making any outsized claims, being careful to note that the benefit of hormones on cognition was "modest" and "the clinical significance of these modest differences . . . is quite uncertain. Data from long-term randomized trials are required before applying this information to the clinical setting."

A later study, printed in the December 2001 edition of *Fertility and Sterility*, found that long-term postmenopausal hormone therapy did have a slight beneficial effect on women's nonverbal memory and attention. Comparing test scores (including those for memory, verbal fluency, executive functioning, concentration, and attention) of postmenopausal women sixty years and older who had and had not been treated with hormones, a team of scientists from the University of

Michigan Hospital and Health Center in Ann Arbor concluded that women who used hormone therapy performed better on prefrontal and executive function tests but not on the others. They emphasized again that the benefit was "slight," noting that "further longitudinal studies appear warranted to assess both the specificity of these findings to those cognitive domains and to determine whether the findings are consistent across socioeconomic groups and educational levels."

Some nine months earlier, the March 21, 2001, issue of *JAMA* [*Journal of the American Medical Association*] published an analysis of studies, performed by Dr. Erin S. Leblanc at the Oregon Health Sciences University in Portland, of the effects of hormone therapy on various memory problems. The article concluded that "in women with menopausal symptoms, HRT [hormone replacement therapy] may have specific cognitive effects." Women who had experienced menopausal symptoms such as severe hot flashes and trouble sleeping were shown on hormones to have improved verbal memory, vigilance, reasoning, and motor speed. The analysis added, however, that for women without menopausal symptoms, there seemed to be little or no benefit from hormone therapy. One possible explanation for these findings is that estrogen products do effectively treat hot flashes, so that for women who haven't been able to sleep or function because of them, relief can lead to an increased ability to concentrate and think. In other words, the studies' positive conclusions about memory may be the by-product of estrogen's effect on other symptoms rather than a direct effect on the brain.

Women who go on hormone therapy programs, without symptoms, often see little to no effect on cognitive functioning. But sometimes the opposite is true. As one such woman said: "I was put on HRT by my gynecologist and I became a medical basket case. Finally I saw a neuropath who 'knew' what my symptoms were before I told him. He said he sees a lot of women with symptoms caused by perimenopause, birth control pills, and HRT. Some of the specifics he talked about were head pains, body pains, numbness of extremities, confusion, depression, fatigue, not being able to think clearly. And my favorite personal symptom—speech problems. I could not articulate, lost words, couldn't finish sentences. My case was extreme, but now that I've stopped HRT, I'm better." In April 1999, *JAMA* published the results of a Yale University study that found that although the brain-activity patterns of women on estrogen more closely resembled those of premenopausal women, there was no difference in memory test scores.

An *American Journal of Epidemiology* study from October 2001 further found no consistent change in cognition test scores between women who did and did not take estrogen. Conducted by Dr. Suzana Alves de Moraes and colleagues from Johns Hopkins University Bloomberg School of Public Health, the study collected data on 2,859 women, ages forty-eight to sixty-seven, who had their cognitive functioning tested twice by a battery of exams given between 1990 and 1998. The researchers wrote that their findings "would seem to indicate that, at least for women in the age range included in the study, use of estrogen replacement therapy is not associated with age-related cognitive declines."

Finally, among the papers published in the February 2003 issue of the AMA's [American Medical Association's] *Archives of Neurology* were two dealing with estrogens—one examining the effects of Premarin [a brand of estrogen] on cognitive functioning and the other assessing the effects on memory of estradiol produced by the body. The first, conducted by researchers at the University of California at San Diego, investigated women with diagnosed AD, all of whom had undergone hysterectomies and thus could be given Premarin alone. Half of those on Premarin took the standard dose of 0.625 mg and the other half took a higher dose of 1.25. Researchers tracked the change in hormone levels as well as periodically administering several different tests for cognitive functioning. Hormone levels increased fourfold in women on the 0.625 dose and eightfold in those on the 1.25 dose. But there were no significant differences in cognitive functioning nor in other neuropsychological measures, compared to the women on placebo, either at two months or twelve months into the study. Similar to the effects of pharmaceutical estrogens, higher natural levels of estradiol do not help older women—or men—perform any better on memory tests, as the second study showed. To the contrary, this study, conducted in the Netherlands, found that women with higher total estradiol levels had poorer memory performance and less hippocampal matter (the hippocampus being the part of the brain responsible for memory). In men, however, there was no association observed between estradiol levels and hippocampal matter, but a trend emerged that linked higher levels of total estradiol with poorer memory performance. According to the researchers, "Our data do not support the hypothesis that higher natural levels of estrogen are associated with better memories." (In contrast to the Netherlands volunteers, who were all elderly people "with no dementia," the volunteers receiving Premarin in the San Diego study all had Alzheimer's—which does impose limitations on the study, because asking women with degenerative memory disease to recall if they've taken their medication is not the best way to collect information.)

## Overhyped Studies

Whatever effect hormone treatments may have on menopausal memory loss, they have no proven effect at all in preventing or treating Alzheimer's disease and dementia, despite the fact that the attempt to establish positive connection got off to a promising start. In 1994, a study of women from the Leisure World retirement community in Southern California announced that those who had taken hormones were a third less likely to develop Alzheimer's disease, the risk falling as the estrogen dosage increased. The study received a massive amount of press; coupled with findings about hormones and osteoporosis in the 1980s, and hormones and heart disease, a new estrogen renaissance kicked into highest gear. Much neglected—one might say "censored"—was a similar study reported on in *JAMA* in May 1993 that found those who took estrogen were more likely to have died of Alzheimer's than were nonusers.

An August 17, 1996, article in the *Lancet* reported that in a five-year study of 1,124 older women, Columbia University researchers discovered that only 5.8 percent of those who took estrogen developed Alzheimer's, compared to 16.3 percent of those who did not, reducing the risk of contracting AD by 87 percent. But in evaluating the study, the *Harvard Health Letter* noted: "A major limitation . . . , however, is how it was conducted: the scientists interviewed the women about postmenopausal estrogen use but had no way of verifying their answers. The resulting information is probably not as reliable as data gathered in a controlled clinical trial, where groups are assigned to different treatments and then carefully watched over time," adding that "the investigation did not look at the most beneficial doses of estrogen, the best formulation or how long HRT needs to be taken." Dr. John Growdon, a professor of neurology at Harvard Medical School, went on to caution readers that "it is probably not a good idea to start HRT solely to prevent Alzheimer's until more information is available."

Another headline-grabbing report lauded as having "tipped the balance in favor of estrogen" was the Baltimore Longitudinal Study of Aging, a sixteen-year study, the results of which were published in the June 1997 issue of *Neurology*. It found that taking estrogens reduced the risk of developing Alzheimer's by approximately 50 percent. Again, health specialists were cautious, reporting that this study, like those before it, was "observational . . . and as such, not ideal. Unlike randomized controlled trials, in which the participants are assigned to follow one course or another and are likely to have similar characteristics, observational studies offer no assurance that the women in both groups began the trial on equal footing."

Despite reveling in so-called positive findings about estrogen and Alzheimer's, scientists found themselves unable to explain how the hormone prevented the disease. They theorized that, like its protective effect on the heart (which was later disproved), perhaps estrogen kept the brain young by shielding existing neurons and encouraging further neuronal growth. The more exposure to estrogen one has, the theory posited, the more consistently one's cognitive abilities would survive.

This hypothetical relationship between estrogen and the brain was challenged in March 2001, when a Dutch study set out to document whether a longer reproductive period, which implies a longer exposure to estrogen, was associated with a lower risk of Alzheimer's. After looking at a population of 3,601 women aged fifty-five and older over the course of ten years, the authors of the study determined that their findings did "not support the hypothesis that a longer reproductive period reduces risk of dementia." In fact, women with longer reproductive periods had a slightly increased risk of developing the disease. Newsletters that relied at least partially on drug company money were quick to add spin on the study, noting that while "natural estrogen didn't seem to protect against Alzheimer's, "ERT [estrogen replacement therapy] might."

More bad news on estrogen and the prevention of Alzheimer's came in March 2001 via the *Archives of Neurology.* Scientists attempting to resolve conflicting findings about HRT's capacity to reduce Alzheimer's risk looked at several communities of women in the United Kingdom. They concluded that "the use of ERT in women after the onset of menopause was not associated with a reduced risk of developing Alzheimer's disease."

## Estrogen as an Alzheimer's Treatment

Findings about estrogen as a preventative measure are clearly inconsistent, but findings about estrogen as an Alzheimer's treatment are almost nonexistent.

In November 1996, less than two years after the Leisure World study popularized estrogen for Alzheimer's prevention, a study was presented that looked at the effect of estrogen on twelve women with Alzheimer's. Scientists found that after eight weeks, the estrogen group performed twice as well on tests as the group not taking estrogen. Once treatment stopped, the benefits diminished, but didn't disappear entirely. Analyzing the study, *The New England Journal of Medicine Health News* commented that "because the study was so small, it's too soon to say whether hormone therapy might be a useful treatment for Alzheimer's," particularly given the fact that estrogen "when used alone as in this study, promotes cancer of the uterus and may increase the risk of breast cancer."

The February 23, 2000, *Journal of the American Medical Association* reported a study in which researchers randomly placed approximately 100 women with Alzheimer's disease on high-dose estrogen, low-dose estrogen, and a placebo. The participants had an average age of seventy-five and all had had hysterectomies. The study, led by Ruth Mulnard of the University of California at Irvine, found that while estrogen improved mental functioning after two months, it did not prevent decline after one year. In fact, the estrogen patients actually showed decline on the Clinical Dementia Rating Scale (CDR) versus those receiving placebo.

Gradually doctors were forced to admit that the outlook for treating Alzheimer's with hormones was bleak. Dr. Kristine Yaffe, an estrogen researcher at the University of California, admitted in 2001 at the annual meeting of the American Association for Geriatric Psychiatrists that "we are less optimistic that estrogen can be used as a treatment for Alzheimer's," but insisted "there is more exciting data on whether estrogen can be used against longtime decline and development of the disease.". . .

Dr. Diana Petitti of Kaiser Permanente observed in a *JAMA* editorial that "prospective observational studies continue to suggest that ERT might protect against cognitive decline and the development of dementia. Data on ERT and HRT to prevent cognitive decline and dementia are not consistent, however, and randomized trials of estrogen in the treatment of Alzheimer's disease show no evidence of benefit."

Another study, by Sudha Seshadri et al., reported in the March 2001 *Archives of Neurology*, drew on a United Kingdom research database of about 220,000 women, the largest study of Alzheimer's and estrogen to date. The conclusion: "The use of ERT in women after the onset of menopause was not associated with a reduced risk of developing Alzheimer's disease."

## Some Reasons for the Estrogen Myth

So given how little evidence there is for using hormones to ward off *or* treat Alzheimer's, how is it that a virtual cottage industry was built to use them for just that? The story encompasses science, health newsletters, and major sources of medical information to equate normal cognitive problems with Alzheimer's disease, a confusion that occurs on many levels, from scientists who use data on one type of memory loss to hypothesize on the other without consistent differentiation, to newsletters (many of which receive drug company dollars) that blatantly confuse one finding with another.

A further distinction should be made between mild cognitive impairment, a clinically defined level of memory loss that is associated with early stages of Alzheimer's disease, and the menopausal memory problems associated with normal aging. According to the *Archives of Neurology*, mild cognitive impairment is a "transitional state between the cognitive changes of normal aging and Alzheimer's disease, in which persons experience memory loss to a greater extent than one would expect for age, yet they do not meet currently accepted criteria for clinically probable Alzheimer's disease." Research has indicated that a certain percentage of individuals with mild cognitive impairment develop Alzheimer's disease, and unlike menopausal or normal memory loss, there seems to be evidence to support a connection between the two. A May 1, 2001, article published in *Neurology* states that people with mild cognitive impairment have about triple the risk of developing Alzheimer's disease. When studies discuss cognitive decline, they are not necessarily talking about mild cognitive impairment; they are usually talking about decreased scores on memory tests.

I found that language is often used to confuse data on cognitive impairment with that specifically on Alzheimer's. One *Johns Hopkins Medical Letter* described the findings of the Proceedings of the National Academy of Science by noting estrogen "might" help improve memory. This weak finding on the role of HRT in slowing cognitive decline is quickly extended to include Alzheimer's: "estradiol stimulated the growth of nerve pathways in cells from a region of the brain associated with the progression of Alzheimer's disease." The finding here was on estrogen and cognitive ability. By suggesting that these findings were in "the same region of the brain as Alzheimer's," they connect the two in the reader's mind. However, unless there is data to suggest a connection, it is irresponsible to infer that the solution to one problem will necessarily cure the other.

Here is the essence of the estrogen experiment. For forty years drug companies, scientists and researchers have been playing carrot-and-stick with women's lives. They hold out poorly substantiated claims for estrogen's health benefits, which buys them time as they try to develop the proof to back up the claims. But the fact remains that after all these years, and with countless deaths attributable to estrogen via cancers, cardiovascular complications, blood clots, and other health problems, including asthma and gallbladder disease, the evidence isn't there. If the data is there, women must demand to see it before agreeing to put more pills into our bodies.

Some recent studies have focused on progesterone and testosterone as Alzheimer's treatments instead of estrogen alone. Again, the facts just aren't there, so women should be wary about these claims, too.

# NANCY'S NEXT CAMPAIGN

Claudia Kalb, Debra Rosenberg, and Julie Scelfo

Embryonic stem cells are cells that have not yet become a particular kind of tissue but have the potential to develop into almost any
of the more than two hundred kinds of cell types in the human
body. Many researchers believe that embryonic stem cells may
have the potential to help those suffering from Alzheimer's disease. Some scientists think that these cells could be transformed
into the neurons damaged by Alzheimer's and then transplanted
into the patient's body. However, research on stem cells is a con-
tentious issue in the United States because stem cells come from
human embryos. Some consider it unethical to experiment on human embryos, which they consider as inviolable human life. In
2001 President George W. Bush limited federal funding of stem cell
research to studies of sixty existing stem cell lines, which had already been harvested from embryos left over at fertility clinics. His
policy prohibited federal funding for research using new cell lines.

In the following selection, Claudia Kalb, Debra Rosenberg, and
Julie Scelfo describe Nancy Reagan's challenge to Bush's policy.
Reagan's husband, former president Ronald Reagan, died in 2004
after a ten-year struggle with Alzheimer's disease. She is committed
to sparing other families the pain of losing someone to the disease.
She believes that stem cell research offers a hope for a cure and is
campaigning to increase federal funding of additional stem cell
research.

Claudia Kalb has been a senior writer for *Newsweek* since December 2004. A former White House correspondent, Debra Rosenberg became deputy Washington, D.C., bureau chief for *Newsweek*
in 2004. Julie Scelfo works for *Newsweek* as a correspondent on society and culture.

One spring afternoon in 2002, eight long years into her husband's descent into Alzheimer's, Nancy Reagan went to her friend Doug Wick's

Claudia Kalb, Debra Rosenberg, and Julie Scelfo, "Nancy's Next Campaign," *Newsweek*,
vol. 143, June 21, 2004, p. 38. Copyright © 2004 by Newsweek, Inc. All rights reserved.
Reproduced by permission.

home in Los Angeles for a Hollywood-style tutorial on stem cells. Along with Wick and his wife, Lucy, both producers, the cast included moviemakers Jerry and Janet Zucker, actor Warren Beatty and Dr. Richard Klausner, now head of global health at the Bill & Melinda Gates Foundation. Nancy Reagan already knew a bit about stem cells —a year earlier, she'd written a letter to President [George W.] Bush asking him to support embryonic research—but she was eager to delve deeper. Together the group discussed the ethics, the politics and the science. "She asked a lot of questions about what [stem cells] were, where they came from," says Klausner. Nancy knew it was too late to rescue her husband [Ronald Reagan, former U.S. president], but she "had a higher purpose," says Wick. "She feels the greatest legacy her family could ever have is to spare other families from going through what they have."

After the meeting, Nancy began making her views known behind the scenes, respectfully but forcefully—calling politicians, conversing with scientists, buttonholing lawmakers at the rare Washington dinner she allowed herself. Then last month Reagan decided to go public at a Juvenile Diabetes Research Foundation gala, and she asked others to join in her quest. "Science has presented us with a hope called stem-cell research, which may provide our scientists with answers that have so long been beyond our grasp," she said. "I just don't see how we can turn our backs on this—there are just so many diseases that can be cured, or at least helped. We have lost so much time already, and I just really can't bear to lose any more."

Nancy Reagan's bold challenge to her own Republican Party and to Bush's 2001 policy on embryonic research was a pivotal moment for stem-cell advocates. For months they had been rallying across the country; with Nancy's support, and now with her husband's death and heroic farewell, they have found fresh momentum. Last week [June 2004] in Washington, 58 senators, including John Kerry, sent a letter to the White House, urging Bush to relax his restrictions on embryonic-stem-cell research. In a radio address to the nation over the weekend, Kerry reaffirmed his commitment to overturning Bush's policy if elected [Kerry was defeated by Bush in the 2004 presidential election]. On the West Coast, meanwhile, Californians for Stem Cell Research and Cures celebrated the collection of 1 million signatures authorizing a $3 billion stem-cell-research initiative to be put to the vote in November. In Boston 1,400 scientists gathered to discuss both embryonic and adult stem cells at a meeting of the International Society for Stem Cell Research (ISSCR), where the embryonic-stem-cell advocate and Republican senator Arlen Specter encouraged them to stand up for science. "We need more political activism," he told the group. "The marvels of modern science should obviously not be shackled." Newspapers ran editorials calling on Bush to honor Ronald Reagan's legacy by revising his stem-cell policy—"George should do it for the Gipper," said one—and a New York congressman introduced the Ronald Reagan Memorial Stem Cell Research Act of 2004.

All of this infuriated embryonic opponents: one senior Republican aide said naming stem-cell legislation after the president, who was ardently opposed to abortion, was "unbelievably shameless." But out of respect for Reagan, the adversaries mostly held their fire. Bush stayed mum, but privately officials said he would not budge on his opposition to destroying human embryos for the sake of science. "No dramatic advance, no scientific development will change the ethical principle" underlying Bush's position, a senior administration official told Newsweek last week. Laura Bush, whose father died of Alzheimer's, made the media rounds instead, gently reiterating the administration's position on stem-cell research without attacking Nancy head-on. "We have to be really careful between what we want to do for science and what we should do ethically," she told CBS. When she was asked if she would endorse additional stem-cell research, the answer was clear: "No."

What is it about embryonic stem cells? How can these microscopic flecks galvanize scientists and celebrities and, at the same time, pit First Ladies against each other and turn political allies into formidable foes? Under the microscope, embryonic stem cells look like luminous stars in a black-and-white galaxy. Just days old, they have the extraordinary capacity to become any one of the more than 200 cell types that make up the human body—from heart to brain to muscle. Researchers believe they may hold the key to curing or at least revolutionizing our understanding of deadly diseases like Parkinson's, diabetes and Alzheimer's. But no matter how mysterious or magical their powers, the cells are culled from human embryos, and to those who consider the fusion of sperm and egg sacred life—whether it takes place in a womb or a lab dish—they are morally off-limits for research.

In an effort to placate both scientists and pro-life constituents, Bush announced a compromise policy on Aug. 9, 2001: federal funds, which underwrite the vast majority of scientific research in this country, could be used to study embryonic stem cells, but only those that had already been isolated in the lab and grown into stem-cell "lines." Almost immediately scientists began complaining that the restrictions would inhibit their work. The administration said as many as 78 lines existed, but that number turned out to be inflated; as of last week only 19 were available. (Other lines exist but can be worked on only with private money.) Scientists say the lines are often difficult to obtain and of questionable quality. "It's like forcing us to work with Microsoft version 1.0 when the rest of the world is already working with 6.2," says biologist David Anderson of Caltech. Without better access to embryonic stem cells, U.S. scientists worry that they're in danger of becoming by-standers to medical innovation.

Political support for embryonic-stem-cell research—galvanized by testimony from scientists and the heart-wrenching stories of sick Americans pleading for cures—has come from surprising quarters. Rep. Duke Cunningham, a pro-life Republican from California, says he is haunted by a child who told him, "Congressman, you're the only person who can save my life." He signed on after a scientist explained that IVF [in vitro fertilization] clinics house thousands of frozen embryos, from which stem cells are derived, and that many are destined to be discarded. "My own personal belief is that I'm actually saving life from something that is not going to be life," he says. Sen. Orrin Hatch, a Mormon from Utah who is staunchly pro-life, is an ardent supporter, too. In early 2003 he, Specter and Democratic senators Ted Kennedy, Dianne Feinstein and Tom Harkin introduced a bill that, with strict regulations, would allow so-called therapeutic cloning to create new embryos from which more stem cells could be harvested. Along the way, Nancy Reagan spoke with both Republican senators and sent Hatch a note backing the legislation. "She's a conservative woman, very much like her husband," says Hatch. "The fact that she's been willing to speak out on this has been very helpful."

Today 4.5 million Americans suffer from Alzheimer's, a number that is expected to spike to 16 million by 2050. Scientists and drug companies are rushing to improve diagnosis and treatment with brain imaging, medications and even an experimental vaccine. But as Nancy Reagan knows better than anyone, available therapies address symptoms only and are unable to halt the ravaging disease, let alone cure it altogether. That's where her passion for stem cells comes in. Already researchers have been able to coax embryonic stem cells into neurons that produce dopamine, the culprits in Parkinson's. Might scientists also find a way to transform them into the neurons damaged by Alzheimer's, then transplant the healthy new cells into a patient's brain? Nobody knows. The reality is that Alzheimer's is so complicated that even miraculous stem cells might not cure it. Harvard neurologist Rudy Tanzi likens the Alzheimer's brain to a defunct stereo. You can't "throw in a bunch of capacitors and transistors and expect to hear music," he says. "You have to rewire the system."

Maria Shriver, whose father has Alzheimer's and who has forged an alliance with Nancy Reagan on stem cells, believes the research could help uncover the illness's genetic link: "It will help millions of children of people with this disease." At the University of California, San Diego, Dr. Larry Goldstein is using embryonic stem cells to develop human brain cells that carry Alzheimer's mutations. Rather than analyze the disease in its later stages, he wants to watch it develop from the beginning, with the hope of creating drugs to stop its progress early on. Ultimately, scientists believe embryonic stem cells will be able to shine a light on the fundamentals of human biology. "It's not just that stem cells will magically cure disease, they can help us understand how life emerges," says stem-cell researcher Ron McKay of the National Institutes of Health. "This is the future of medicine."

When stem cells are involved, however, the future of medicine is never just about medicine—it's about politics, too. Scientific studies become ammunition to support a particular viewpoint; medical data, no matter how nuanced, get spun with political finesse. Now adult stem cells, derived from mature human beings rather than days-old embryos, have become pawns in the debate. The administration and right-to-life groups praise their potential, offering them up as equally powerful as embryonic stem cells, if not more so. Several years ago, research backed those claims, suggesting that adult stem cells were indeed far more "plastic" than anyone had dreamed. But now some scientists are challenging those findings. "People are starting to realize that the science of plasticity is not all there," says Dr. Leonard Zon, ISSCR president.

Unlike embryonic stem cells, adult stem cells are prewired to become a particular kind of tissue—skin, intestine or blood, for example. Like theatrical understudies, they stand in the wings, rushing in only when cells need replenishment after injury or disease. Scientists know the most about the adult stem cells of the blood, which are given in bone-marrow transplants to patients with cancer or blood diseases. That success prompted researchers to wonder: could adult blood stem cells have the same acrobatic ability as embryonic stem cells? Dr. Markus Grompe, of Oregon Health & Science University, initially thought yes. In 2000 he reported that adult blood stem cells were able to turn into liver cells in mice. But two years later Grompe reassessed his data and came to a different conclusion: the blood cells had fused with existing liver cells—more a case of biological identity theft than transformation.

New studies are now questioning earlier work on heart disease, too. In 2001, news that adult bone-marrow stem cells had become cardiac muscle in mice spurred great hope, even leading to clinical trials in humans. Dr. Piero Anversa, of New York Medical College, worked on the original research and stands by it "1,000 percent." But in April two groups reported that they could not reproduce the finding, a critical step in the validation of science. "Our paper says it doesn't work," says Stanford University's Dr. Irv Weissman.

The holy grail for many scientists is a cure for type 1 diabetes, the disease that plagues Doug Wick's daughter and helped spark Nancy Reagan's interest in stem cells. For years researchers have searched for adult stem cells in the pancreas, hoping such cells could make themselves into insulin-producing beta cells, which diabetics lack. But last month Harvard biologist Doug Melton dashed the hopes of many when he reported that he could find no adult stem cells in the pancreas at all. His conclusion: "If you want to make more beta cells, the place to look is embryonic stem cells."

Stem-cell science is still early in development—too early to make absolute statements about what works and what doesn't. Even the most passionate supporters of embryonic research believe the study of adult stem cells should proceed with equal vigor. Embryonic stem cells are the gold standard in versatility, but adult stem cells still hold promise, especially for repair within their own tissue family. A patient with Alzheimer's might benefit from a transplant of adult brain cells from a healthy donor. Or perhaps one day in the future, a drug might be able to jump-start sleeping adult stem cells in a patient's own brain, spurring them to fix the damage. What the scientists want is for the politicians to stay out of their petri dishes.

Back in Washington, the political future of stem-cell medicine remains unclear. Last month Bush's domestic-policy adviser reiterated the president's stance in a meeting with Reps. Diana DeGette and Michael Castle, bipartisan architects of a House letter signed by more than 200 members urging Bush to relax his restrictions. This week, *Newsweek* has learned, NIH Director Elias Zerhouni will sit down with them as well. "It's my hope that the president will revisit the issue," says Specter. Now that the week of Reagan mourning is over, the opposition is likely to take its gloves off. Republican Sen. Sam Brownback of Kansas, who authored a bill banning all forms of cloning—including for stem-cell research—will hold hearings next week on adult stem-cell research, a meeting postponed in honor of Reagan's memorial. "There will be plenty of support for President Bush to continue the policy he has," says American Values president Gary Bauer. The White House, meanwhile, was working hard to downplay the differences between Nancy Reagan and the president. "Reasonable people can disagree," said one senior official.

Nancy Reagan knows she may not get what she wants on the first try, but Ken Duberstein, her husband's former chief of staff, says she won't give up. "She's not backing off," says Duberstein, "because this can be a living legacy of Ronald Reagan." And as Nancy herself has said, she doesn't have time to lose.

# CHAPTER 4

# CARING FOR ALZHEIMER'S PATIENTS

# FAMILY CAREGIVER STRESSES

Victoria M. Hogan et al.

The following selection is an excerpt from a study conducted by Victoria M. Hogan and her colleagues on the experiences of in-home caregivers of people with Alzheimer's disease. Hogan and her colleagues found that caregivers often experience feelings of guilt and frustration. The caregivers find themselves having to take responsibility for helping the loved one with all the tasks of daily life, including bathing, dressing, and feeding. As more and more of their time is spent caring for an Alzheimer's patient, caregivers have less time for other relationships. The authors also discuss caregivers' methods of coping. For example, caregivers describe the usefulness of support groups and the value of having the support of other family members. The researchers suggest that occupational therapists could play a key role in helping caregivers and recommend that entrepreneurial therapists develop programs to help the families of Alzheimer's patients. Victoria M. Hogan is an occupational therapist at Western Pennsylvania Hospital in Pittsburgh.

Alzheimer's disease afflicts approximately four million people in the United States. It is estimated that more than seven out of ten people with Alzheimer's disease live at home. Often it is necessary for family members and friends to assume caregiver roles. Evidence suggests that the amount of time caregivers spend caring for the individual with Alzheimer's disease strongly influences their experience of stress, leading to feelings of isolation, general strain, and disappointment.

The onset of Alzheimer's disease can cause magnification of preexisting family problems or require reorganizing financial arrangements, which can lead to other crises and stress in the family. Neglect and/or abuse may surface if community resources are not adequate. The availability of community and health care resources affects the quality of the caregiving situation. . . .

When individuals assume caregiving responsibilities, their participation in previous roles and routines is likely to change. [B.] Chenoweth

Victoria M. Hogan et al., "Role Change Experienced by Family Caregivers of Adults with Alzheimer's Disease: Implications for Occupational Therapy," *Physical and Occupational Therapy in Geriatrics*, vol. 22, 2003, pp. 21–41. Copyright © 2003 by The Haworth Press, Inc. All rights reserved. Reproduced by permission.

and [B.] Spencer conducted a study to explore the experiences of families from the earliest recognition of their loved ones' symptoms of dementia and throughout the course of their illness. The most common problems found by caregivers at home were physical and emotional strain, an inability to get away, and concern over finances. A [2001] study by [M.M.] Neundorfer et al. found that acceleration in caregiver depression is predicted by an increase in patient dependency in instrumental and basic activities of daily living. [B.] Bergman-Evans suggested caregiver depression is significantly related to self-assessed health status and days missed from work. [G.A.] Hills found more research needs to be done to determine the needs and perceptions of caregivers and the effect of caregiving on role performance. . . .

## The Study's Method and Participants

The purpose of this qualitative study was to explore the phenomenon of role change as experienced by in-home caregivers of individuals with Alzheimer's disease. Examining the ways in which a caregiver's role changes may allow occupational therapists, and other health professionals, to gain a greater understanding of the caregiving experience. This may help in the development of effective strategies for helping caregivers cope with their activities, and ultimately allow them to perform these tasks with greater ease and satisfaction. A reduction of caregiver burden may also help preserve the emotional satisfaction caregivers and their loved ones obtain from their relationships.

Prior to the initiation of the study, investigators obtained approval from the Institutional Review Board (IRB) at the researchers' university.

Data collection with caregivers was conducted through the use of open-ended questionnaires, support group field notes, and individualized semi-structured interviews employing phenomenological techniques. The Role Change Assessment (RCA) 2.0 was used to gain preliminary information about caregivers, from which individualized semi-structured phenomenological interviews were designed. Phenomenological interview techniques seek to obtain the perspective of the person being interviewed. In phenomenological interviews, questions may begin by saying "tell me about . . . ," or "describe to me. . . ." The phenomenological researcher uses probes, such as "tell me more about that," to gain further elaboration when interviewees reveal particularly relevant information.

Study participants included a purposeful sample of persons of any age and either gender who at the time of the study were serving as in-home caregivers of individuals with Alzheimer's disease. Caregivers were unpaid family members and were to have been living with care recipients for a minimum of six months from the time the recipients symptoms of Alzheimer's disease began. The researchers felt that a minimum of 6 months of this type of caregiving was necessary for gaining more accurate information about the phenomenon of caregiver role change. Thirteen participants were recruited from Alzheimer's disease support groups in western Pennsylvania; one participant was a personal contact of one of the researchers; and one participant was obtained from a professional referral source. All fifteen caregivers completed questionnaires. All participants spoke fluent English and were capable of giving informed consent. Two of the caregivers were husbands of care recipients, while six were wives, five were daughters, one was a son, and one was a sister. All of the responses to these fifteen initial questionnaires were later analyzed as part of the thematic analysis process. . . .

## Study of Caregiver Stress

Six themes relating to caregiving responsibilities and role change emerged from the data analysis. Three of the themes are further divided into more specific sub-themes.

## Feelings of Guilt

The majority of participants expressed considerable decline in leisure role participation because they needed to be with their loved one or because they felt guilty leaving that person. The caregivers expressed they did not want to burden other family members while they participated in leisure roles. Participant D emotionally commented:

> It's like you raise a family, and then you are thinking you can do what you want, and I am back to square one . . . I feel guilty leaving her with my husband all the time because it is my mom . . . (Crying) . . . so that is the hard part.

Participant F flatly stated:

> My activities . . . are affected because I just can't just get up and go. I have to plan ahead.

The caregivers expressed that they no longer had the time to participate in leisure activities due to their caregiving responsibilities. There was one atypical case identified during the interviews in which leisure participation increased. One possible explanation for this phenomenon is that he appeared to be using leisure as a means of coping with the stress of caregiving.

## Feelings of Role Reversal

*"I Feel Like the Parent."* The caregivers in our study frequently expressed that the dynamics of their relationships with care recipients had significantly changed since they had become caregivers. Analysis of interview transcripts revealed several types of changes. In the situation where the caregiver was a son or daughter, a common characteristic was a feeling of role reversal. When asked to describe her current relationship with her mother, Participant D tearfully stated:

> Well, now, it is kind of like parent and child, and I feel like the parent . . . (crying). Sometime(s) I feel like she is supposed to be the mom and I'm the kid, and it will never be that way again. So it is hard.

The caregivers also articulated sadness over changes occurring in their loved ones that prohibited them from interacting with them as they previously had. One participant described the current relationship as "changed more to mother/son than wife/husband." During the in-depth interview, Participant H expressed sorrow over the loss of her mother as a confidant:

> Before I was more able to communicate with her, telling her things, talking together . . . (I feel) very sad. Because it is not that you only lost a friend . . . the feelings are not the same.

The interviews demonstrated that caregivers often felt that the quality of the interactions with their loved ones had declined. Feelings of anger, frustration, sadness, resentment, and grief were frequently noted. The caregivers described the difficulty they had in accepting these changes. Participant B stated:

> I would get angry at him, shout at him, swear at him, trying to get him to be his normal self. Of course that is not possible. I just did the best I could. It is tough when somebody you love isn't there anymore. Like the guy at the last support group, said, "My wife died." Essentially that is what my father has [done]. He is not there anymore, even though he is here . . . After nine years, all I do is see him like he is now. And so, it is no longer a viable thing to remember him.

## Having to Do Everything

*"I Do Everything."* A significant change found in the majority of relationships was that the caregiver was now responsible for assisting the loved one with activities of daily living. These tasks included personal hygiene, bathing, dressing, toileting, feeding, and medication management. Participant D compared her mother's prior level of assistance to her current status:

> I used to go to her house and I would help her get into the tub, but then she was on her own. I would wait around and do things, then I would go back when she was ready. But, now I'm actually getting her in. I'm right in there . . . then I get all the clothes and bring them up and get her out and help her dry. Same with her hair. I comb her hair. I do everything. She likes brushing it, but it's not right.

Participant F described her assistance to her husband:

> Before, I would get up and take care of myself. Now I get up

and make sure he showers, shaves . . . I lay out his clothes for him and make sure he gets dressed. Then I can tend to myself. Then I come downstairs and make his breakfast, put it on the table, and then make my breakfast. The rest of the day he sits on the porch or in the house, but it is the same thing. He is taken care of, and then I take care of what I have to do.

## Methods for Coping

All interviewed caregivers described methods to help them cope with the stress of caregiving. The most commonly discussed strategies resulted in sub-themes of support groups, self-education, faith, assistance from others, and regulating daily routines.

*"Go to a Support Group."* A significant number of the caregivers verbalized the importance of the support group in helping cope with the stress of caregiving. The support groups provided ideas on how to handle situations, as well as the support of being with people who were experiencing similar situations. Participant B repeatedly articulated:

> The only thing you can do is go to a support group . . . there is nothing out there to tell you what to do or how to do it. Go to a support group. Take what they go through or what they have gone through, and adapt that to what you are going through. There is no other way to learn to take care of someone with Alzheimer's. At least, I knew of nothing, and I still don't think there is anything out there other than support groups that gives you a guess on what to expect.

*"It's Really Been . . . a Form of Education."* Many of the caregivers spoke of their desire to find information about Alzheimer's disease and caregiving. This quest for knowledge resulted in taking classes, reading books, and attending seminars on these subjects. Many expressed frustration at the lack of information available for caregivers, as well as the need to seek out this information. Participant A stated his frustration:

> It's really been a challenge and a form of education. Who needs all this education at my age? It's a part of life.

*"I Definitely Need God's Help."* Reliance on faith was a reoccurring coping mechanism found in interviews and support group discussions. A number of the support groups the researchers attended had clergy as guest speakers. Discussions took place regarding how reliance on faith could help them cope. Participant H stated:

> I don't know how I have the strength to do this, I just pray to God everyday.

Participant A also demonstrated his increased reliance on faith by expressing:

> I definitely need God's help in regards to keeping the patience,

love, and knowledge in how to handle these situations.

*"Without the Support . . . There Would Be No Way."* Participants frequently mentioned that caregiving without outside assistance would not have been possible. They turned to neighbors, spouses, children, grandchildren, siblings, friends, and community resources for assistance. These people helped by providing paid or non-paid respite care, assisting with household responsibilities, taking responsibility for some of the care recipient's activities of daily living, and being confidants and sources of support. Participant D stated:

> My husband is great. He never minds being with her [mother with Alzheimer's disease]. Without the support of the family, there would be no way. And the day care center of course. I had to have that.

Participant H described her sources of support in the following manner:

> (My support is) . . . my family and my friends at work. They tell me ideas and they try to tell me how I have to do (things) with my mom . . . Or the doctors at work. They give me advice. They tell me things. They are a big help.

Participant B described his reliance on his neighbor for assistance in caring for his father:

> I check on him first thing in the morning, and the lady across the street comes over and gets him up and dressed, or gets him showered and his breakfast.

Participant C agreed with her husband (Participant B) on the importance of their neighbor in caring for her father-in-law:

> We have been so lucky to have her (neighbor) . . . I mean, if we didn't have her, we wouldn't be so well.

## The Need for a Routine

*"Now It Is Much More Regulated."* Many of the caregivers described the importance of having a regulated daily routine. This involved keeping the individual with Alzheimer's disease in a familiar environment, following the same schedule everyday, and planning ahead. When asked how she coped, Participant H stated:

> I have to keep my schedule always the same. I know where I put things. I know what I have to do, and how I have to do it. I just do it automatically.

Participant D described her schedule in the following manner:

> Now it is much more regulated. I can't just make the short little trips like I used to because I have (my mother) with me all

the time. I am also working full time now, so that doesn't give me as much time either. It's getting myself ready and her ready . . . I am waking her up. I am getting two people dressed instead of just one and then I drop her off at the center on my way to work, go to work, pick her up after work . . . I don't have the freedom I used to have.

## Increased Household Responsibility

A frequent finding was a change in the household management role. Participants reported having more household responsibilities, but less time to do them. Caregivers were responsible for tasks such as cooking/ meal preparation, washing dishes, laundry, errands, cleaning, and driving. These tasks often dominated their days. Participant H described her household management responsibilities in the following way:

I have to leave everything ready. . . . The syrups, the juices, her medication. I make her lunch or dinner. I have to have everything ready for her before I leave. I have to cook, I have to clean . . . I am always busy.

The caregivers were now often responsible for performing tasks that were previously done by the individual with Alzheimer's disease. Participant A described a typical day:

I am basically doing the same thing I did 2 or 3 years ago, but it is involving more doing things around the house that she basically used to do. She is doing very little of this, such as cooking meals, doing dishes, and doing laundry.

Another spousal caregiver, Participant G, stated:

He can't help with anything anymore, so it is pretty much that I do everything. . . . He thinks he is helping me, but he is not. He does not get the dishes clean, so I have to watch everything that he does and must make sure the dishes are clean. Most of them I have to do over again. So, he is hardly a help at all.

## Loss of Friends

*"Some People . . . Don't See Us Anymore."* Not only was the quality of the caregivers' interactions with the individuals affected, but their relationships with others changed as well. One individual wrote that since her husband has had Alzheimer's disease, her interactions with others have "become increasingly different. Some people shy away and don't see us anymore." Similarly, Participant E discussed how she and her husband no longer participated in their former social circle due to her husband's inappropriate behavior, which in turn affected her relationships with these people. Participant D described her interactions with her siblings as almost exclusively about the care of their mother.

*"We Can't Do That Anymore."* A frequent discussion topic during interviews and support groups was having less time for social interactions due to caregiving responsibilities. Caregivers felt they were spending less time with their children, grandchildren, and friends. As Participant G stated:

I used to go and play cards a lot. [My husband] will go with me. So I don't go a lot because I don't think he'll enjoy it. We used to do the bulletins for the church and we can't do that anymore. It's just that I have so little time with everything else I have to do.

Participant F regretfully articulated these feelings as well:

[My relationship with my daughter has changed because] I don't get to see her as much anymore. I used to see her every week.

*"It Is Their Mom, Too."* The topic of the caregivers' desire for additional family support was discussed during multiple support groups and interviews. The caregivers lamented that they experienced stress, while family members not living with the individual provided very little assistance. Participant D, who was caring for her mother, hesitantly said:

I do sometimes wish that I would get more help. . . . I wish other family members would volunteer instead of me asking. I know if I asked, they'd help, but I feel like, why do I have to ask? It is their mom too. I feel like everyone else has gone on and nothing has changed for them. But for us, everything has changed.

Participant G expressed frustration over her husband's sons not assisting in his care:

It is very disappointing because when I ask, they say, "Oh yes, we understand. We'll be up to help." Not once, not once have they helped. And I asked them in July. Two and a half months ago.

## Decreases in General Health

Caregivers frequently described a decrease in their overall health. One caregiver explained: "My time spent in maintaining health and wellness has taken a back seat to his care and well-being." Another individual wrote on the questionnaire: "My time for my own needs of health care come after his needs." The health and wellness of the caregiver was also a common topic at support group meetings, with group facilitators often emphasizing the need for caregivers to take care of themselves.

Some of the caregivers reported being on medication for depression and/or anxiety. Others reported being on blood pressure medications due to their stress levels. Participant A described his mental health:

> I would say for the last six to nine months I have been having more typical and emotional depression and anxiety, due to the fact of caregiving. I've had problems in this way . . . I had to go to the doctor and get different medications. . . .

## The Role of Occupational Therapists

This investigation has demonstrated how caregivers often find it difficult to fulfill the duties and responsibilities of their chosen life roles, due to the demands of helping others. Often caregivers do not have the time or energy to devote to their own health and happiness. Occupational therapists can help resolve this problem by placing more emphasis on assessment of family and caregiver needs. Such assessment will illuminate the challenges faced by individual care providers, and may indicate the need for caregiver support. Caregiver assessment strategies are in need of further development both in home care and in other community and institutional settings. This includes informal interview and observation techniques as well as more formalized evaluation tools.

Occupational therapists may also be pivotal in recommending valuable strategies to improve caregiver role performance and quality of life. These include making recommendations for support group involvement, counseling and/or medical services, and health and wellness programs. Occupational therapy entrepreneurs may also consider developing their own community wellness programs, of which caregivers may be participants. There are many options for expanding the interaction between therapists and caregivers, and they are only limited by time and creativity. The economic, medical, and social benefits that can be reaped from acknowledging caregiver needs and promoting healthy caregiver role performance cannot be understated.

# Ethical Concerns in Treating Alzheimer's Patients

Gunilla Nordenram

In the next selection Gunilla Nordenram describes her experience performing dental work on an Alzheimer's patient. Nordenram tells her story to illustrate that the negative behavior of Alzheimer's patients is usually the result of their suffering from pain, which they cannot verbalize. Nordenram warns that it is difficult to judge the appropriate levels of care required when patients are unable to express their needs. She explains that a caregiver such as a dentist faces an ethical dilemma in deciding how to treat a patient who is unable to give informed consent. Such caregivers must try to balance a patient's need for optimum treatment with a patient's need for autonomy and dignity, she writes. Gunilla Nordenram is an associate professor and course coordinator of geriatric dentistry at the Institution of Odontolody, Karolinska Institutet in Sweden.

Dementia may be defined as an acquired global impairment of intellect, memory, and personality, but without impairment of consciousness. Many types of dementia disorders exist, of which Alzheimer disease (AD) is the most common. AD involves serious communication problems, speech being limited to a few words or incomprehensible sounds. If behavioral and psychological symptoms in dementia occur, aggression, shouting, anxiety, and hallucination become particular problems. It has been shown, however, that persons in a severe stage of the disease can still react to various stimuli and experience uncomfortable sensations. . . .

Although cognition and social behavior in moderate and severe dementia are impaired, the afflicted patients have a rich and powerful emotional life. Loss of intellect is not loss of personhood. Decisions regarding treatment needs and the management of treatment must attempt to maximize the patient's quality of life and improve safety. An often overlooked area is oral care.

Gunilla Nordenram, "The Ethical Challenge of Treating Pain in Alzheimer Disease: A Dental Case," *Ethical Foundations of Palliative Care for Alzheimer's Disease*, edited by Ruth B. Purtilo and Henk A.M.J. ten Have. Baltimore, MD: Johns Hopkins University Press, 2004. Copyright © 2004 by The Johns Hopkins University Press. All rights reserved. Reproduced by permission.

The oral region is a "private" zone of the body. Entrance to the mouth is restricted to persons who are near and dear to us and to certain professionals (e.g., dentists, dental hygienists, speech therapists, and physicians). Personal space in terms of the oral region varies from person to person—whether a friend, an acquaintance, or a stranger, and in this hierarchical scale, enemies are far away. Elias Canetti talks about teeth as an instrument of power or a weapon, not just a biological part of the body, and asserts that the teeth are the armed guardians of the mouth.

For a newborn baby, the sucking reflex is vital for its survival, notwithstanding that nowadays we can feed a baby artificially through a tube. When we touch the cheek of a newborn, the baby turns its head toward the touched side—the orienting reflex. For a tiny infant, feeding also means close contact with the caregiver and the first opportunity to establish confidence and nonverbal communication. In the late stage of dementia, the sucking reflex and the orienting reflex have returned, and the oral zone may be as significant for the severely demented person as it is for the newborn baby.

When persons suddenly become afraid, they often put their hands in front of their faces, instinctively and immediately guarding their mouths. The aggressive behavior of persons with AD in oral care situations may be an expression of fear caused by a lack of understanding of what is going on and of why people want to look into their mouth. They feel that the private oral zone has been invaded, arousing emotions that the patient can no longer interpret or verbalize. The most natural reaction in this situation is to hide the mouth or forcefully reject any attempt to enter it.

However, refusal behavior in dental care can also mean something else. As an illustration, I describe one of my patients, Cathy, whom I met in about 1990. When I first met her in the hospital, she was aggressive, restless, and agitated. She screamed, bit, and fought whenever anyone tried to open her mouth.

## Cathy's Life History

Cathy's life is a living illustration of modern European history. She was born in Saint Petersburg, Russia, at the beginning of the last century, into a wealthy family. She was brought up by a private governess, learning several languages and how to play various music instruments, to embroider, to manage a household—all the things that a fine young lady needed to know at that time.

She married young. In her thirties, her husband was executed by the Stalin regime. She managed to leave the Soviet Union and settled down in France. After World War II, she remarried, taking as husband a French diplomat. They lived in various parts of the world and her knowledge of languages was very convenient. Her husband's last post was at the French embassy in Stockholm, and when he retired they remained in Stockholm, living in a large apartment in the city center, in a district where such accommodation is now very expensive.

Cathy's husband died a few years after his retirement, and Cathy had been a widow for more than twenty years. She had no children and gradually reached a situation where she was quite alone. She had no relatives or friends left and no social contacts. Only rarely did she let anybody into her flat. An exception was one of the neighbors, who enjoyed her confidence and used to help her in emergencies (e.g., by changing her lock after she had lost her keys). In fact, this had happened quite often lately.

## Changes in Behavior

In May 1990, Cathy's neighbor contacted the district nurse about this elderly lady. He thought something was wrong with her: she was behaving strangely from time to time. Recently, she had gotten into the habit of walking around the city at night with 100,000 Swedish crowns (US$10,000) in her handbag and carrying all her antique and expensive jewels in a plastic bag. She could easily have been robbed, but she was lucky. She was unable to find her way home. Even in dark city streets, she stood out from the crowd—the police had learned who she was and they drove her back to her flat on several occasions.

After the call from the neighbor, the district nurse and a geriatrician visited her. That day she was in a good mood and let them in. The flat was rather untidy. There was a smell, especially from the kitchen. But one does not go into people's homes in order to inspect them, so the visitors simply took note of all this and wondered how Cathy coped when it came to eating.

Cathy seemed to spend her time looking at old photos and drawings from Saint Petersburg. The old lady still gave off an appearance of high class; she was mobile and seemed in good health. She denied having problems with her memory or any other problems. At that time, she spoke Russian fluently, French, and rather good Swedish. The only thing she complained about was her neighbor who used to help her. In a whisper, she insisted that he was a secret agent, presumably a KGB officer. She obviously suffered from paranoid delusions. She was offered help from the municipal care for the elderly, but she was not interested.

## Diagnosis of Alzheimer's

A few months later, her neighbor heard screams coming from her flat. She was found lying on the floor with a femoral neck fracture and was taken to the hospital for surgery. She was examined and tested for dementia and the assessments indicated severe AD. In addition, she was no longer able to walk and sat in a wheelchair. She was completely uncooperative, angry, agitated, and rather aggressive. It was considered necessary to place her in a unit for the demented and she was put on continuous heavy medication with neuroleptic drugs. She was admitted to a hospital for long-term care, where I was the hospital dentist at the time.

By now she had lost her Swedish and her French. With the assistance of a Russian interpreter, the nurses tried to find out what she was saying with the few words she used, often in a screaming voice. The interpreter said they were better off not knowing what Cathy was screaming, because it consisted only of swearwords and abuse. She was very uncooperative, and dependent in all her daily activities, apart from eating, when she used her hands, instead of utensils: she had totally lost her table manners. Despite heavy sedation, she still showed aggressive and hostile behavior, and the ward staff found it difficult to take care of her. Naturally, she did not allow anyone to brush her teeth. She bit and screamed and forcefully rejected every attempt to approach her face.

## Caring for Cathy

Cathy seemed to have healthy teeth as far as the staff were able to judge. I was asked to examine her teeth, and it was not easy—I was able to take only a brief look. There seemed to be a lot of caries, and some molar teeth had fractured crowns with sharp edges. Her oral hygiene had been rather neglected. A second treatment attempt with heavy sedation and an interpreter present also failed.

We (the ward nurses, the doctor, and myself, the dentist) concluded that the patient could be in pain from her teeth. However, an assessment, including an X ray, determined that dental treatment could be carried out only under general anesthesia. The patient had no relatives, only a guardian—a bank clerk who took care of her finances. As far as her dental treatment was concerned, he said that we could do whatever was needed, money was not a problem. So the treatment decision was discussed and made with the consensus of the physician, the ward staff, and me. We thought it was neither fair nor beneficial for her to have toothaches, and that this could affect her quality of life. The dental treatment should be in accordance with "science and approved experience" as supported in the Swedish Act of Supervision. The treatment was aimed at making the patient feel as comfortable as possible.

One month later, the oral treatment was performed under general anesthesia. In the meantime, Cathy had fractured the crowns of her upper central incisors, and suddenly she lost the appearance of a person with healthy teeth even when viewed from a distance. The X rays, taken when the patient was asleep, revealed a large amount of infection. The only possible treatment was extraction of all teeth and roots.

Some days later, I was contacted by the doctor, who was rather upset that all of Cathy's teeth had been extracted. Cathy was also quite black and blue after the extractions, although it looked worse than it was. After the doctor had looked at the X rays, she understood the treatment decision and accepted it as the only course of action. Healing was normal.

Three months later, the doctor asked me to make dentures for Cathy. I considered such treatment to be quite useless, but the doctor insisted, and I agreed to try. Cathy now seemed to be calm, but I was unable to get a response from her. I decided to start with an upper denture to see if it was possible. The patient was not exactly in a cooperative mood, but she was not actively refusing treatment. The ward staff wanted Cathy to have new teeth to make her look prettier: they really cared for her.

However, when the denture was ready and in place in her mouth, initially she was not at all interested in looking at her face in the mirror. According to the nurses, Cathy became really pretty with her new teeth, but after eventually looking into the mirror for a long time, she took out the denture and placed it on the table in front of her. She did not want it. We were the ones who wanted her to have new teeth. If her attention was distracted, she seemed to forget her new denture and could wear it for several hours, but from time to time she would remove it from her mouth. She did not want to use it.

Oral pain and discomfort were the cause of the refusal behavior in this AD patient. She felt pain but could not interpret the signals and need for adequate treatment. Her reaction was aggressive, with screaming and biting whenever anyone tried to look into her mouth or feed her with warm or cold food. After the healing of the lesions following the tooth extractions, her heavy medication with neuroleptic drugs had been totally discontinued. Her aggression and irritability had completely disappeared. Of course, she was still severely demented, but she looked and behaved as though she was satisfied— and she got her good table manners back. She was much easier to care for, and the ward staff were happy.

## Issues with Patient Consent

We find Cathy's accusing her neighbor of being a secret agent and her going out at night with her jewels and money to be curious and irrational. Considering Cathy's earlier life, she and her former husband had undoubtedly encountered spying, and she had escaped from Russia with some of her belongings in a bag. Her behavior was rational in that context, but not in her then-current life situation.

As the AD progressed, she gradually lost her acquired languages and reverted to her mother tongue, which is common in persons with dementia. Living as an immigrant or in a foreign country, as Cathy was, a person with dementia becomes even more confused when verbal communication fails, due to the cognitive impairment suffered.

Cathy was brought up as a fine lady and was taught good table manners as a child. When she got rid of her oral pain, she was able to behave properly in mealtime situations. The importance of this for Cathy is impossible to know, but with her background it might well have been a dimension of dignity for her to eat with instruments as she was used to that helped her to remain integrated and as active as possible.

The ethical dilemmas facing the people who cared for Cathy were paternalism, beneficence, autonomy, and informed consent. Balancing her individual autonomy with the caregivers' desires to protect cognitively impaired persons from harm and provide optimum treatment is difficult. It is an obligation to choose the alternative that best satisfies the patient's need for integrity and dignity.

Informed consent is the formalized process of protecting patient autonomy, and the person is supposed to understand the burdens and the benefits of the treatment. Caring for patients with cognitive impairment requires evaluation of the patient's ability to participate in the treatment decision. . . . If the dementia patient has a diminished decisional capacity or is not competent to reach rational decisions, in Sweden the care requires the involvement of a proxy decision maker. "Living wills" are rare in Sweden, and not legally binding within the Swedish context. The advocate for a patient with AD in a dental treatment situation may be a relative, the hospital staff, and the dentist, working in consensus. The treatment philosophy must be tempered by considerations of burdens and benefits of the treatment for patients—that is, acting in the patients' best interests. Human dignity must be respected, and care must be beneficial and of good quality.

## Making Treatment Decisions

Chemical or physical restraints, even general anesthesia, as in Cathy's case, may be necessary. This burden, including a possible postoperative period of confusion, must be weighed against the benefit provided by the treatment. In Cathy's case, the benefits of the tooth extractions turned out to be relevant, although the new denture was of no use to her. This treatment was too much, even though it brought minor harm to her.

The strain experienced by the dentist in coping with patients with AD is similar to that experienced by nurses and informal caregivers such as relatives. Dentists, like other providers of care, must understand and perceive their dementia patients as unique and valuable human beings, including the patient's premorbid life and current situation.

The assessment of treatment need for patients with severe dementia must take into account not only such factors as autonomy, benefit, and relief of pain, but also include the caregivers' insight into the person behind the diagnosis. Cooperation between a number of categories of caregivers—both the various professionals and the nonprofessional caregivers such as family members and friends—is necessary.

Fair and proper oral care for patients with dementia is resource demanding, and this becomes especially obvious in times of constraints on public funding. Justified and respectful care for older people requires careful consideration of care needs in clinical situations and in policy. In the face of health and welfare cutbacks in the public sector, it is a challenge to argue for adequate resources for irrational patients such as cognitively impaired people. Care is a moral project, and the challenge is based on a belief in mankind and the concept of intrinsic human dignity. In our diversified world, with rapid changes in technology and economic situations, shifts in contemporary biomedical ethics are evident. An ongoing dialogue of biomedical ethics is therefore essential. It should be based on actual practice with authentic cases that augment and extend the notion of good and bad, right and wrong, within the professions as well as within society as a whole.

# DRUG THERAPIES FOR ALZHEIMER'S DISEASE

Josh Fischman

> As the population of elderly people in the United States grows, more and more people are suffering from age-related diseases such as Alzheimer's. Thus it becomes ever more important to learn more about the treatment and prevention of these diseases. In this article Josh Fischman describes some of the research that has been done on drugs that can be used to treat Alzheimer's. He also points to the fact that many patients' symptoms, such as irritability and agitation, are often ignored and left untreated. He suggests that drugs can be effective in treating these symptoms. Josh Fischman is the deputy editor of the health and medicine section of *U.S. News & World Report* in Washington, D.C.

Imagine: Inside your head, your memory is a dark, vast lake, and the waters are receding. Ripples that used to lap steadily on shore, bringing with them the time of day, the names of coworkers, and the location of your car keys, now barely reach. As the waters retreat farther, they take with them your ability to count, to drive, and to recognize the face of your wife or husband. Soon the lake is but a distant, dim shadow, holding words you can no longer speak and bodily functions you can no longer control. You are kept from it—from what used to be you—by an impossibly wide stretch of exposed and featureless sand.

For people with Alzheimer's disease and their families, this shrinking lake is not just a metaphor but a painful reality. "Time is what this is all about," says Pierre Tariot, an Alzheimer's specialist at the University of Rochester Medical Center in New York and now a caregiver as well. "If my father-in-law knows how to flush the toilet and where to poop for another nine months, that's huge for our family."

## Buying Time for Alzheimer's Patients

Tariot and other researchers are combining new and existing therapies to buy as much time as possible, staving off brain failure for months and sometimes years. Last week [July 2004], at the International Con-

Josh Fischman, "Vanishing Minds," *U.S. News & World Report*, vol. 137, August 2, 2004, pp. 74–78. Copyright © 2004 by U.S. News & World Report LP. Reprinted with permission.

ference on Alzheimer's Disease and Related Disorders in Philadelphia, scientists showed for the first time that a drug could slow the deterioration from mild cognitive impairment to full-fledged Alzheimer's. Other drugs can reduce the agitation and irritability that comes with the disease, keeping patients out of institutions. This reflects a growing awareness that Alzheimer's is more than memory loss; it is a syndrome of psychiatric disorders as well. New brain scans are making earlier, clearer diagnoses possible, and very early experiments point to drugs that may limit Alzheimer's-related brain damage. A novel regimen of task-training, reported just last month, showed that people with mild Alzheimer's could still learn new skills. "We have to attack Alzheimer's in multiple ways," says Steven DeKosky, director of the Alzheimer's Disease Research Center at the University of Pittsburgh. "We have no trouble doing this with cancer. But now we're learning to apply this many-pronged approach to Alzheimer's, too."

Along with the hope, there's stark reality. Drug benefits are still modest. And there's been gloomy news on the prevention front: Vitamin E and the heart drugs called statins, which had shown some promise in reducing the risk of Alzheimer's, have flunked their most recent tests. And hardly anyone at the Philadelphia meeting was talking about magic stem cells: Though they received a burst of publicity in the wake of President [Ronald] Reagan's death from complications of Alzheimer's, the cells seem more appropriate for treating other brain disorders.

All this is playing out against a drumbeat of increasing urgency, as the disease makes inroads against an aging society. The rate of Medicare beneficiaries with Alzheimer's more than tripled during the 1990s, and the number of sufferers is projected to balloon from the current 4.5 million to 16 million by 2050. "Remember, for baby boomers in this century the average age of death is 85," warns Tariot. "At 85, the chance of Alzheimer's is almost 50 percent. So look to your right and look to your left. One of those two people will probably get it."

Getting it later, not sooner, would be an improvement, of course. For many people, a condition called mild cognitive impairment, or MCI—you forget things regularly, but your judgment and reasoning are intact—is a precursor to Alzheimer's. So Ronald Petersen of the Mayo Clinic took about 750 people with MCI and put some of them on Aricept, a common Alzheimer's drug, and some on a placebo. At first, he reported in Philadelphia, fewer people in the Aricept group developed Alzheimer's. Unfortunately, the rates evened out at the end of an 18-month period, so Petersen described the study as encouraging but no more than "a foot in the door."

## Disappointment in Aricept

It was also a small boost for Aricept, which works by limiting the destruction of a neurotransmitter, acetylcholine, in the brain. It's the most frequently prescribed Alzheimer drug, but a recent study in the medical journal *Lancet* questioned its value. After following over 500 Alzheimer's patients for three years, the study reported those on Aricept ended up disabled or in nursing homes just as often as did those on a placebo. The research has generated a strong reaction. Sam Gandy, an Alzheimer's researcher at Thomas Jefferson University in Philadelphia, points out that the study showed Aricept did have some early benefits, delaying cognitive decline. Others are even more optimistic. Says Rachelle Doody, director of the Alzheimer's Disease Center at Baylor College of Medicine in Houston: "Other studies show the disease can be stabilized, often for years, with treatment. I can't emphasize that enough."

## The New Drug Memantine

For more severe cases, the newest kid on the block is memantine, sold as Namenda and approved last fall [2003] by the Food and Drug Administration. In tests in people in later stages of Alzheimer's—when patients lose the ability to dress or clean themselves—the drug slowed their decline by 50 percent. Again, this benefit generally lasted for no more than a year. Memantine works on a different principle than Aricept, inhibiting a chemical that overexcites brain cells, leading to cell damage and death. Because of that, says Barry Reisberg, a psychiatrist and Alzheimer's specialist at New York University, it lends itself to combination therapy: "It's likely that doctors will be giving cocktails of Aricept and memantine to their patients." Indeed, a study that paired the drugs showed that not only did patients' cognition stabilize for six months, but their temperament—their levels of crankiness—improved as well.

Patient agitation and irritation are a huge and neglected aspect of Alzheimer's. "The public thinks Alzheimer's is a memory disease. But, in fact, there are lots of neuropsychiatric symptoms," says Constantine Lyketsos, a psychiatrist at the Johns Hopkins University School of Medicine. "Apathy, depression, agitation are the most common problems." Adds Reisberg: "Alzheimer's patients often develop delusions. They think their family is stealing things from them, for example. And they get very aggressive and irritable towards their spouse." That kind of behavior, studies have shown, hastens patients down the road toward institutionalization, since families can't cope with it.

The agitation often starts as patients get frustrated with themselves, as simple memories start slipping away, says Janelle Lafser. Her husband, Frank, was diagnosed with Alzheimer's in 2002, at the unfortunate early age of 53, but began having problems several years before that. "We'd have a date to meet someone, and he'd come up and ask me what time we were leaving the house. I'd tell him. And then 20 minutes later he'd come up and ask me again," says Janelle, of La Quinta, Calif. "I'd tell him, and then 10 minutes later it would happen again. And again. I'd get irritated, and he'd get agitated." Frank started having trouble doing the household bills, got seriously depressed, and told Janelle, "I just can't do it anymore." A former executive at Sherwin-Williams, he declined to the point where he couldn't hold a job mixing paint at a local hardware store.

## Help for Agitation and Irritation

Fortunately, there have been some real advances in the treatment of agitation, depression, and other symptoms in people with dementia. Doctors have tried using traditional antipsychotics, but they have unpleasant side effects like heightened cholesterol levels and movement difficulties akin to Parkinson's disease. Worse, recent studies have indicated a higher risk of stroke. In Philadelphia, Tariot presented the results of a trial of a newer drug, quetiapine, sold as Seroquel. In a 10-week study of about 300 patients in nursing homes, the medication reduced agitation and aggression by about 20 percent, but with few of the side effects seen in other drugs. The medication also alleviated depression. The National Institutes of Health is currently sponsoring a longer trial of the drug, along with another medication called risperidone and several other antipsychotics. The results should be available next year [2005].

## The Importance of an Accurate Diagnosis

But drugs are only useful with an accurate diagnosis. For the Latsers, that diagnosis came courtesy of a PET scan of Frank's brain. Because he started showing problems at such an early age, doctors didn't think Frank had Alzheimer's. They diagnosed serious depression, but antidepressants were no help. His performance on cognitive tests—remembering shapes, repeating lists of words—didn't fit the standard Alzheimer's profile. Finally, Janelle insisted on a PET scan, and it showed reduced activity in brain regions typical of Alzheimer's. "It's devastating to hear that, but it also felt like a ton of bricks being lifted off my shoulders," says Frank. Janelle noticed the difference immediately. "He stopped blaming himself. And I stopped being angry with him, because I realized it's not his fault."

"PET is a direct way to look inside a person's skull to see activity, more direct than a battery of psychological tests," says Daniel Silverman, a brain-imaging specialist at the University of California–Los Angeles. The scan measures the energy used by brain cells; damaged cells, in an Alzheimer's patient, use less energy, and the loss usually shows up in particular brain regions. Standard neurological workups are highly accurate—on the order of 90 percent—but when PET scans are added to standard tests, the rate of missed Alzheimer's diagnoses falls from about 8 percent to about 3 percent. PET scans also help doctors distinguish Alzheimer's from other types of dementia, another study has shown. Such results recently prompted the federal government to announce its intention to expand Medicare coverage to PET scans for Alzheimer's testing.

## A Step Backward

The news about preventing Alzheimer's, however, is not as good. Statins, the cholesterol-lowering drugs, had been linked to a lower incidence of Alzheimer's in several small studies. Researchers speculated that the drugs prevented some inflammation in the brain that led to cell damage. But in Philadelphia, data from three trials that followed about 8,300 people for several years showed no protective effect. Says Doody: "I see patients who come in who have statin prescriptions purely for their Alzheimer's. We have no evidence to support this. Nor evidence supporting antioxidants." Petersen's study of MCI patients also looked at the effects of the antioxidant vitamin E and found no benefit.

So most of the new hopes center on new approaches to therapy. One drug, called Alzhemed, appears to reduce levels of the protein beta-amyloid, which forms the plaques seen in dying regions of the brain. But no one has yet shown the drug eliminates the plaques, or if it slows or prevents actual memory problems. Another compound, an antibody to beta-amyloid, does appear to reduce plaques—but only in three patients so far. And again, this may not affect the course of the disease. Researchers think it will be at least six or seven years before they have better answers. "These are promising avenues," says Reisberg. "But we just don't know where they are going to take us."

# HOW GRANDDAUGHTERS COPE WITH THEIR GRANDMOTHERS WHO HAVE ALZHEIMER'S

Kellee Howard and Jerome F. Singleton

Alzheimer's has a serious impact on family members, even those who are not involved in the direct care of the patient. The following selection is an excerpt from a study of granddaughters whose grandmothers suffered from Alzheimer's. Researchers Kellee Howard and Jerome F. Singleton found that granddaughters of Alzheimer's patients commonly experienced a feeling of embarrassment, which they coped with by avoiding their grandmothers. Some of the granddaughters also experienced guilt that they might not be helping their mothers enough with many of the daily responsibilities of caring for their grandmothers. The granddaughters also felt sad in remembering how their grandmothers had been before the disease took hold. The researchers found the more information the granddaughters had about Alzheimer's, the better they were able to cope with the stress of having a grandparent with the disease. Kellee Howard is a project manager with Medtap International, Inc., in Bethesda, Maryland. Jerome F. Singleton is a professor at the School of Health and Human Performance at Dalhousie University in Halifax, Nova Scotia.

When a parent assumes the caregiving responsibilities of someone with Alzheimer's disease, the relationships between family members, as well as the family roles, may be altered. The caregiving role is generally assumed by the female within the home; a daughter or daughter in-law. The children of the caregivers are affected as their mother becomes involved with the caregiving responsibility of their grandparents with Alzheimer's. The leisure patterns of the family are affected as the grandparent's behavior and daily care affect the everyday routines of the family. The focus of this research was to gather information to generate new insights about how granddaughters were affected when their grandmothers had Alzheimer's disease. Information was collected by interviewing six granddaughters. The themes that emerged from the granddaughter's stories included problems with social interaction and feeling of embarrassment due to the grandmothers' behavior. Stress and tension, feelings of guilt, feelings of sadness, feelings of frustration and anger also emerged. Avoiding the caregiving situation, participating in activities, the need for possessing information about Alzheimer's disease and the importance of support were other themes that emerged. . . .

## The Background of the Study

When disability strikes one member of a family the homeostasis of the family may be affected. If the person with a mental disability is residing within the home there is often additional strain on families. [L.S.] Noelker and [S.W.] Poulshook (1982) reported that primary caregivers felt that the interpersonal relations of household members may be relatively unaffected by the presence of a physically disabled elder whereas a mentally impaired elder may affect the roles and relationships existing within the family. Family members see their relative transform from a physically healthy, alert loved one to a confused, helpless stranger. This stressful, non-normative life event may spill over and affect the entire family system.

Caring for a person suffering from Alzheimer's disease is a challenge that may change the pre-existing roles of the family, including the various communication and behavior patterns that have previously existed. Despite the consequences, many family members are willing to endure the considerable personal and economic sacrifices to care for their relative with dementia. These sacrifices are often assumed by the women within the home.

The caregiver struggles to meet the needs of the person with Alzheimer's while trying not to abandon their care and responsibility to other family members, including their partner and any children residing within the home. Some family members may resent the fact that the primary caregiver's attention is monopolized by the person with Alzheimer's disease. Consequently, the caregiving strain placed upon the female is experienced by all family members in some form.

Specifically, grandchildren may be affected by the presence of the person with dementia. [E.] Brody (1989) explained the relationships between families caring for other members and described how teenage daughters cared for their grandmother but complained about all the responsibility. For the children spending time with their friends became a rare event where participation occurred only on certain occasions. It no longer became a decision or choice. Children frequently complained that they were embarrassed to entertain their friends at home due to the unpredictable behavior of the person suffering from Alzheimer's disease. [E.] Brody (1989) states:

"It isn't fair," they said. They (the children) can't even bring friends home because the behavior of the elderly woman is disruptive and embarrassing. A granddaughter is tearful. She cannot bring her suitor home because the grandmother makes embarrassing noises.

Many of these children are pressured into growing up at a faster pace than other children. Children have to cope with this new lifestyle by using individual strategies that may result in a variety of responses. One 13-year-old daughter was reported as "having no social contact with classmates and developed fantasy friendships with her stuffed animals and referred to herself as her mother's caregiver" [according to (G.R.) Hall, (B.) Buckwater & (J.) Crowe, 1990].

## Research Question

What was the impact a grandmother with Alzheimer's disease had on a granddaughter?

## The Method of the Study

The focus of this investigation dealt with the family relations and the caregiving experience, qualitative research was the chosen methodoloy. [R] Bleiszner and [L.] Shea (1987) report that "qualitative research methods are especially appropriate in cases in which the area of interest cannot be adequately understood outside of its natural setting, such as in the leisure context." Qualitative methods invite hypothesis development, enabling researchers to discover the nuances of the interactions between family members. This type of analysis will allow the voices of those living the caregiving experience to be heard. It seeks to discover the realities, relevant contexts and intrinsic and extrinsic effects associated with caregiving on family relationships. . . .

This form of inquiry allows the researcher to uncover what is going on, rather than assuming what should be going on (Stern & Pyles, 1985).

The sample for the study, was to be solicited through a local Alzheimer's Society. However, after the pilot interview was completed the investigation used the snowball technique enabling the initial participant to recommend potential participants for the investigation.

All participants were between the ages of twenty-one and twenty-seven, they were all female and their grandmothers had Alzheimer's disease. The sample for this investigation consisted of six participants and at this time the themes became repetitive. Due to the difficulty in gaining access to a sample, three of the participants were sisters living in the same household and three were unrelated. All participants had grandmothers with Alzheimer's disease; however, each family had different characteristics associated with their grandmother.

The sample varied due to the length of time the grandchildren resided at home, the state of the disease the grandmother was in, the primary caregiver, five participants' mothers and one participant's aunt assumed that role. However, the similarity of having a grandmother with Alzheimer's disease enabled related themes to emerge.

The gathering of information was done in the form of interviews. An interview guide was used for assistance in helping the participants express their feelings. It consisted of a series of open-ended questions. By asking the participants open-ended questions, it allowed them to express feelings that close-ended questions would not have achieved. The interview guide was, however, loosely followed and not all questions were asked. The interview took on the form of a conversation with the interviewer only using the guide to probe the participants when the respondents were having difficulty expressing themselves. The interviews were taped, but were erased after transcription occurred. The interview took place at a time that was convenient to both the subject and the researcher. Four of the interviews took place in the participant's home. One occurred at her place of work and the other location was one that the participants had suggested, her mother's school. These were all informal settings and were suggested by the participants. Each interview varied in length ranging from forty-five minutes to one hour. . . .

The initial interview was seen as a pilot interview which allowed the researcher to become familiar with the interviewing technique. However, it proved to be a very useful interview and was therefore used as part of the data. Each interview was transcribed verbatim as it allowed the researcher to become thoroughly familiar with the information. Once the third interview was completed, certain themes began emerging. . . .

In the beginning of analyzing the data, the researcher began to code data using a word search mechanism available on the computer. Once the data was coded from each interview, it was placed into categories on a separate file. This file contained a mixture of quotes from participants which all shared common code words. These words were then placed in categories and were analyzed for similarities. As the interviews were transcribed the themes emerged. . . .

## Grandmother's Behavior

A basic theme that repeated itself throughout the study was the grandmother's behavior. This unpredictable behavior led each granddaughter to experience problems with social interaction. Each granddaughter complained of having to explain to her peers about her grandmother's behavior. When planning for a party or even having a group of friends over, the presence of the grandmother was always cause of concern. Concessions often had to be made if a large number of people were visiting.

Guilt was another emotion that was discussed by some of the

granddaughters. Some dealt with it better than others as was evident in the results. Guilt was also felt by other family members especially the primary caregiver who tried to divide her time between the grandmother and other family members. This guilt was transposed onto the granddaughters as they saw their mother burdened with the caregiving responsibility. They expressed feelings of guilt because they felt they may not be assisting their mother in the responsibilities that she dealt with on a daily basis.

As a consequence, feelings of frustration and anger often developed as a way to express these feelings of guilt. This flow of emotions from guilt to frustration to anger contributed to the granddaughter's experiencing feelings of stress and tension. The unpredictable behavior of the grandmother only intensified these emotions and, in turn, contributed to additional stress and tension resulting in a continuous cycle of emotions.

Feelings of frustration were also felt by some family members when other family members refused to acknowledge and/or avoided dealing with Alzheimer's disease in any manner. Even when family members acknowledged Alzheimer's disease, the granddaughters often found that relatives interfered with caregiving role, especially when their involvement was on a short term basis.

During the interview process recalling these situations brought on another set of emotions. Some of the granddaughters remembered their grandmothers before they began to suffer from Alzheimer's disease. Recalling some of these memories caused some of the granddaughters to feel sad as they compared her previous behavior with them. Even those granddaughters who did not recall their grandmothers before Alzheimer's disease had displayed itself, remembered uncharacteristic actions or remembered them displaying the forgetfulness that is characteristic of the disease and consequently sadness was felt. The ability to cope with the caregiving situation revealed various coping behaviors. Depending upon what mechanisms were used, some granddaughters had greater success in dealing with their grandmother having Alzheimer's disease. Some granddaughters avoided the situation entirely and ignored the grandmother's behavior; others withdrew from their surroundings.

## Information and Coping

As other coping mechanisms emerged, a link was observed between the amount of information that the granddaughters possessed or were exposed to, and how they coped with their grandmother's disease. One of the granddaughters attributed her grandmother's condition and her ability to deal with her behavior to her mother who was very outspoken about Alzheimer's disease.

Other granddaughters would partake in various activities to get away from the frustrations they experienced at home. Some granddaughters found participation in physically challenging activities relieved tension; others found peace while participating in more passive activities. This was a coping mechanism that the granddaughters frequently discussed.

Another technique that affected how the granddaughters coped with their grandmothers was the presence of support. This was not always a positive experience. Family support was cited as being very important by all granddaughters. Unfortunately support from relatives may be more of an aggravation than an assistance, especially if it is sporadic and uninvited. Other families had support from their relatives which was unavailable to both the primary caregiver and the family.

The granddaughters expressed gratitude for having other family members present, to share the responsibility as well as the experience. Friends often added support, someone to talk with and rely on for emotional support. Granddaughters discussed this type of support as being important for them in dealing with the Alzheimer's disease experience.

Yet even friends sometimes do not understand the emotional torment that caring for somebody with Alzheimer's disease has on a family. All of the granddaughters agreed with the need for some form of support whether it is formal or informal.

Feelings of frustration seemed to be closely related to how the granddaughters coped with the various situations that they experienced on a daily basis. When the grandmothers' behavior exhibited signs of unpredictability and their behavior became annoying, some of the granddaughters became frustrated and angry.

Once they realized the underlying cause of the grandmother's behavior was a result of Alzheimer's disease, some of the granddaughters displayed feelings of guilt, as previously shown. . . .

## Areas for Further Research

This investigation indicated that a granddaughter's life undergoes an alteration when faced with experiences related to their grandmother having Alzheimer's disease. This was the overall theme that presented itself throughout the investigation. Even though the family situations were all different and the ages of the participants varied, the emotions that were expressed and the coping strategies that were discussed revealed common themes.

The participants in this study who were between the ages of twenty-one and twenty-seven, indicated that the grandmothers' unpredictable behavior led to embarrassing situations that they tried to avoid, especially when they were interacting with their friends. They also indicated that various coping strategies were beneficial in dealing with the Alzheimer experience. This included participation in leisure activities which allowed the granddaughters to escape the Alzheimer experience and to relieve frustration and anger; the benefit of having information about Alzheimer's disease; and the importance of positive support. This investigation helped to reveal information for future researchers to use in studying how other cohorts of grandchildren may be affected when a grandparent has Alzheimer's disease.

This investigation allows future researchers to build upon the information that was revealed to create new avenues of research. For example, other cohorts of grandchildren such as teenagers and young children may be investigated to reveal the problems that they encounter and examine the similarities or differences between the cohorts. Another area of research may include investigating male grandchildren and their reaction to a grandparent with Alzheimer's disease.

This investigation presented the groundwork for research into areas such as the importance of support systems and their availability to grandchildren; the importance of educating children about Alzheimer's disease in the schools so they may become aware of its presence; and the importance of leisure activities for grandchildren in coping with having a grandparent or parent having Alzheimer's disease.

# Writing Therapy for Alzheimer's Patients

Alan Dienstag

In the next selection, Alan Dienstag describes a writing group that he and author Don DeLillo led for two years for a group of people in the early stages of Alzheimer's disease. Dienstag writes that DeLillo helped him realize that writing is a form of memory. This revelation was his impetus for starting the group. Dienstag describes the great satisfaction the writing group gave its members as the writing activities reminded them of what they could still remember and share. The group eventually disbanded as the participants became sicker. However, they had created a collection of writing to safeguard their memories for their families and friends. Alan Dienstag has a private practice in New York City, where he works with adults and teenagers in individual and group psychotherapy. He is also a consultant and support group leader supervisor for New York chapters of the Alzheimer's Association.

Few illnesses inspire the kind of dread as that caused by the prospect of Alzheimer's disease—which is understandable. For people in the early stages of the illness who are experiencing impairments but still entirely cognizant of the dissolution that lays ahead, the challenge is to construct a life in the shadow of an advancing darkness: to answer the question, "What is the point?"

Professionals working to improve the lives of people in the early stages of Alzheimer's disease should be able to fashion a meaningful response to this question. The difficulty lies in the fact that despite our best efforts, our attention is continually drawn to the unraveling taking place before us. The individuals' strengths and character, the very core of the person with whom we are interacting, seem to recede.

As we watch our clients lose their memories, powerful feelings surface that have a profound effect on how we think about our work. These feelings can narrow our field of vision in ways that are often insidious and make it difficult to think creatively about possibilities. This was the first among many lessons I learned through my experi-

Alan Dienstag, "Lessons from the Lifelines Writing Group for People in the Early Stages of Alzheimer's Disease: Forgetting That We Don't Remember," *Mental Wellness in Aging: Strengths-Based Approaches*, edited by Judah L. Ronch and Joseph A. Goldfield. Baltimore: Health Professions Press, 2003. Copyright © 2003 by Health Professions Press, Inc. Reproduced by permission.

ence with the Lifelines Writing Group.

As someone who has run support groups for people in the early stages of Alzheimer's disease since 1995, I did not think I needed to be convinced that valuable psychological work could be done with people in the early stages of the illness. I saw firsthand that, allowing for modifications in the process, the benefits of supportive group psychotherapy for people with serious medical illnesses could be extended to people in the early stages of Alzheimer's disease. With these groups, individuals were not only supported but also encouraged to grow. I was resolute in encouraging group members to resist being defined by what they could *not* do and inspired by their valiant efforts to find meaning and purpose in their lives. Despite this, my sense of the therapeutic possibilities available for these people now appears to have been limited in some important ways.

## Writing Therapy

In the spring of 1996, I got a call from the director of the local Alzheimer's Association chapter. She told me that a member of a caregiver support group was married to a writer who wanted to speak with someone about using writing as a therapy for people with Alzheimer's disease. She asked if she could give him my name and number. I agreed but was not enthused. I thought that this was not a good idea and would be unlikely to succeed. The activity would be too frustrating, too dependent on an interest in writing, too solitary, and so forth. I was also not excited about having to explain all of this to someone who was surely well intentioned but, in all likelihood, naïve and unrealistic. When I realized that I was going to be speaking with Don DeLillo, a highly acclaimed and renowned author, I was more intrigued but still unconvinced. We discussed the difficulties and, in the course of our discussion, Don said something that sparked my curiosity. He talked about the experience of writing as a more concentrated type of thinking. "Writing is a form of memory," he said.

*Writing is a form of memory.* The phrase stayed with me for some time. I repeated it to myself and told it to others with whom I worked. I realized that for all of my work with people with memory impairments, I had thought very little about memory. To the extent that I thought about memory at all, it was in fact about the *loss* of memory. It had never really occurred to me to think about other forms of memory and the possibilities inherent in them. It was a writer's insight on the nature of memory that suggested these possibilities, and although I still had only a vague idea of how we might put them to work, I saw the potential and committed to working out an intervention plan with Don.

## The Intervention Plan

We agreed that working in a group would reduce some of the pressure on any particular member to perform. We also agreed that the group would be neither a class nor a therapy group per se. Writing would not be taught or critiqued and written self-expression would be valued above all else. Don and I would function as co-leaders, providing support and encouragement as needed. I believed that the writing should be done during the group time and left with us at the end of the session. This took the burden of locating and remembering a notebook every week from the participants and their family members. It also freed the group from the onus and pressure of assignments. Group members would write and read their work to one another and discuss whatever came up in the process.

As with all successful collaborations, ours had many advantages that could not be designed or "worked through." Don, who was shy and reserved by nature, was perfectly content to let me "run" the group. This is not to suggest that his role was less important. Don contributed to the group in a way that was uniquely suited to his identity and expertise; he was critical to its success. If I had run the group by myself, it would have inevitably evolved into writing as *therapy*, but Don's involvement guaranteed that the focus on writing would be maintained. His belief that people need stories to live, and his appreciation of the unique value of writing as a means of expression, elevated the group members' efforts.

In our group, my clinical sensibilities and Don's creative sensibilities intermingled. The group's functioning was more of an intuitive and creative process than existed in other groups I had led. Don had no interest in "teaching" writing, and I was not inclined to run a traditional therapy group as long as he was around. Our primary focus was on making people comfortable and structuring the group so that people would be inspired to write. The fact that I was making no effort to place the work of the group into some kind of traditional psychotherapeutic framework enabled me to see and understand my work with group members in a fresh way.

Our goal was to stimulate memories and feelings. We began by devising a list of topics, one or two of which we would present at each meeting, which might serve as a point of departure. The original list was made up of the following subjects/titles:

- I remember . . .
- My friend
- An unforgettable person
- The house where I grew up
- Summer memories
- The last time I saw . . .
- The ocean
- What is happening to me
- Birthdays
- My doctor
- A movie

- My mother's voice
- My father's hands
- A photograph
- What other people notice
- A precious object
- The future
- My life now

Group members were free to reject these and choose their own, ask for another suggestion, or not write at all. We followed a strict no-pressure policy. Don came up with the official name of our undertaking: Lifelines: Alzheimer's Narratives. Over time, this changed to The Lifelines Writing Group.

The criteria for inclusion in the group were as follows:

- Confirmed diagnosis of Alzheimer's or related dementia
- Awareness and understanding of the diagnosis
- Sufficient physical stamina to participate in a 90-minute group
- Sufficient cognitive and language abilities to communicate and to form relationships with other group members as well as to understand the rules of the group
- Willingness and ability to write (potential participants were asked to write "a few sentences" about their day or a favorite activity in the screening interview)

## Creating the Lifelines Writing Group

Our first efforts at recruitment through announcements in the Alzheimer's Association newsletters and in the local paper were not successful. Very few people called, and those who did were interested in activities for individuals who had not yet been diagnosed with Alzheimer's disease or whose illness was more advanced. Initially, we hoped to reach out beyond the relatively small group of people already being seen in early-stage support groups. It became clear, though, that for many people among the population from which we were recruiting the idea of writing "in public" was intimidating. Consequently, we turned to two support groups in the New York City area and focused our efforts on them. We were able to easily recruit six group members from these two groups and set a date to begin.

Offering the group to people who were already support-group members turned out to have significant advantages. The screening process could be streamlined, and the group members' familiarity with one another helped them to relax. An interesting synergy developed between the two experiences. They were distinct but also complementary. Group members often would continue a discussion that had begun in their support group in our writing group. We used these themes at times to generate subjects for writing. Group members also reported feeling a deepening sense of understanding and connection with their writing colleagues to their support group leaders.

The first topic we presented to the group, and one that we returned to several times, consisted simply of two words followed by ellipses: "I remember. . . ." Here is what group members wrote in response (spelling and punctuation are verbatim):

- From Ron, a 68-year-old who spoke very little in his support group:

I remember how nervous I'd been at various times in my life—for no reason at all. I remember how so few of them ever came to fruition.

- From Elizabeth, a 73-year-old retired nurse:

I remember when I was a little girl sitting under a tree during the eclipse. It got dark and the birds went to bed.

I remember that I want to make a boke of what I have things that I have had in my life.

I can remember picking a fig from a tree in Athens. My lover watched me with delight.

- From Charlotte, an 84-year-old:

I remember the first time I walked with my parents on the bridge that went to Brooklyn. It was hard for me and I fell very often. My father would pick me up and carry me for a while and put me back to walk. It took a little time to learn to walk all the way but I did. I remember as I write this about the cat that lived with us who also like to walk and when he saw us ready to go he was right with us and we loved it.

I carried a love for walking all through my life, and even now when things go bad I walk and things seem to get better.

I hope I'll be able to walk as long as I live.

- From Sarita, an 86-year-old retired psychotherapist:

I remember when Poppa's horse brought him home and Poppa having fallen back in his seat. I heard Mamma's outcry as she rushed out and maybe brother Lou was there or brother Nat—because he was brought in and laid on the bed in the downstairs bedroom. Mamma gathered all us kids together and sent us down to Mrs. Carr's house which was always so clean and neat and we spent the night there.

The next morning we all returned home and I looked out of the bedroom sitting room window I think I saw a hearse going down the street. But I was really happy because someone had left an orange and it was all mine.

From the outset, I was surprised at the directness and poignancy of the work produced by the group. I shared the writing with the co-leaders of the support group to which many of the writing group members belonged. These co-leaders were struck by the amount of feeling in the work and by the ways that the writing presented new facets or information about people that they had come to know quite well. The writing seemed to open a different door into the lives of these people.

## The Success of the Group

Very quickly, the group settled into a comfortable pattern of working, in which we would meet, talk together about what was on people's minds for a time, and then write and read the work.

Interestingly, in the moments when the group would fall silent and settle into writing, my own memory was often stimulated. I remembered schoolmates, childhood friends, and visits with long-forgotten relatives. The setting very powerfully evoked in me positive recollections of being in a hushed classroom and concentrating on an assignment. I recalled vividly the quiet pleasure of thinking and the comfort of the group quietly thinking together. This was a particular kind of quiet that I had not thought of in many years, and it was the sound I heard when the writing group did its work.

One important aspect of memory and group dynamics that I had overlooked in my work with these people prior to this experience was that many things are transmittable within groups. This includes everything from feelings to coughs. Although I am very familiar with emotional contagion in the group setting, I had never thought of how this might also apply to the mental activity of writing and remembering. We tend to think of these activities as solitary, and often they are, but the effect of group contagion operates here as well. When individuals are around others who are doing a writing and remembering activity, this serves as a powerful inducement to do it themselves.

## Writing and Remembering

How does understanding this phenomenon translate into helping people who are forgetting? One answer that emerged from the Lifelines group is that we should surround people who are forgetting with *acts of remembering*. People in the early stages of Alzheimer's disease are in danger of forgetting that they can still remember, as are those of us who work with people with Alzheimer's.

Writing and remembering became the work of the group, then, and once the routine was established and a level of acceptance and security had been reached, group members took to the task with surprisingly little resistance. Often, individuals requested help spelling or finding a word. Occasionally, a group member would laugh or start to cry while writing, and of course some participants became frustrated when words and thoughts that once flowed became tangled and confused or stopped altogether. When gentle encouragement failed to help, I sometimes offered to have a group member dictate his or her thoughts to me or I would just write words that would help the person remember a story to tell us. Stories written or told with great difficulty were almost always worth the effort. A particular example of this was the work of a woman named Charlotte, mentioned previously.

## Charlotte

For many years, Charlotte had written a column that appeared in the newsletter of a Jewish women's organization and was especially distressed by the loss of her writing abilities. Charlotte had joined our group with a good deal of apprehension. She had been with us for 1½ years (during which her abilities declined steadily) when we asked group members to write something that would be entitled "My Doctor."

Charlotte struggled mightily to write the following in an almost indecipherable script:

My Docter

*My life if my life was growing in going to going—*

My mother lost her first darghter when she was one hear and when I was born mother watched me although all the time.

*I reamontay when my brother and I bash my mother called the Docter and up the six flights and said was very sick My parents worred a lot and the Docter soften his and said do worred she will life for all time.*

Charlotte fought despair with every word and gave up repeatedly, trying to read and explain her story to the group. Eventually it became quite clear what she was writing about. Her story was about her mother's fear over losing another child, the impact this had on Charlotte and her brother, and her gratitude to the doctor, whose voice she still remembered softening as he reassured her mother that she was fine and would live for a long time. "I was glad for that voice," she said with a smile. After reading the story she went on to explain that she and her brother did everything they could to conceal any sign of illness from their mother. This piece of information certainly helped me understand her stubborn unwillingness to consult with a doctor at various times over the 2 years that she was in the group. More important, it was a heroic act of recollection and self-expression at a level of emotional connectedness and specificity that was not readily available in other ways.

Charlotte's spontaneous verbal contributions to the group were growing infrequent at this point in her participation; yet here was an essential part of her life story that she was able to reconnect to and to communicate to us through the act of writing.

## Writing Can Allow Remembering

Through group members' participation and attendance, I realized that they looked forward to our meetings. They expressed surprise at what they remembered and satisfaction that they were part of such a group. The writing seemed not to remind them so much about what they could *not* do, or if it did, this awareness did not predominate. Of course, there were those for whom the frustration was too great, and even among those who participated eagerly, the time came when they could no longer write well enough to continue.

As the group flourished, I began thinking more about the nature of the experience and ways of explaining it. These musings led me to think about my own grandmother who had died shortly before we started the Lifelines group. When she reached a certain age, my grandmother started giving her possessions away. This was imperceptible at first but became obvious over time. It got so that I had to think twice before admiring anything of hers or even glancing too long at something lest I be required to take it with me.

Occasionally I would protest—but it was of no use. Her determination and the obvious pleasure she derived in this giving away were too great. She would say things such as "I want to *see* you enjoy this . . ." or "I want you to have this now." The objects she gave me covered the full range of the old-closet spectrum: a jazzy black suit of my grandfather's that fit me perfectly, cufflinks and studs inlaid with opaque reddish earthen stones, dishes and servers of every description, lamps, sea shell–encrusted salt and pepper shakers with missing shells, and dusty bed sheets deeply yellowed at the creases from being folded for 35 years. What she gave was what she had saved, and this was their value.

As she neared the end of her life, my grandmother seemed to understand that if you can give something away, you don't lose it. This, as it turns out, is as true of memories as it is of objects and is yet another aspect of memory that is often overlooked. Memories are, in a sense, fungible. Writing is a form of memory, and unlike the spoken word, leaves a mark in the physical world. As a form of memory, writing creates possibilities for remembering, for the sharing and safeguarding of memories not provided by talking. The writing group gave memory back to its members. They were transformed in the experience of writing from *people who forget* to *people who remember*. A member of the writing group once said that when the group was together ". . . we forget that we don't remember." This is a statement of cure, not of the biological and cellular disorder, but of the human disorder, the disorder of loss of personhood brought about by Alzheimer's disease.

If the writing gave memory back to the group members, then the reading—the moment at which the entire group would fall silent and listen—returned something equally essential: the power to give. The thought content of people in the later stages of Alzheimer's disease is described in clinical terms as "impoverished." Alzheimer's disease is an illness in which the losses accumulate moment by moment and day by day. Giving reverses the tide and represents a refusal to be defined by loss. Members of the writing group regularly enriched themselves by giving to one another their most precious possessions.

As the writing became more difficult for group members, yet another important transformation took place. We began to re-read the old work and it became clear that in most cases, the members could not recall having written it and would not likely recall what they had written about spontaneously or be able to write about it with the same richness as they had in the past. We took great pleasure in this reading and in the re-discovery of old memories, however. Here was recollection in the literal sense of the word, a reclaiming through writing and reading of lost parts of the self. "I haven't thought about that in 40 years!"—how often we heard these or similar words while running the group, and what a deep sense of accomplishment and satisfaction they inspired in all of us. During these moments of writing and reading, long-lost memories of friends and family, strangers encountered on trips or at crucial moments, once-precious objects, feelings of joy and sorrow, lessons learned, all became threads of the fabric of life that sprang back along with individuals' sense of self.

## A Fitting End

After operating continuously for 2 years, the group appeared to have run its course. Illness and cognitive deterioration were taking their toll. It became harder and harder to get the group members to write new material, and when they did, they wrote much less. We thought inviting family and friends to a reading would be a fitting end to our work together and the group members supported the idea wholeheartedly. The group members could not choose which stories to read from among the many they had written and asked me to make the selections. Prior to our final meeting, I collected their stories and bound them in a book with their names inscribed on the front. When we met for the last time as a group, I returned their memories to them and watched as they leafed through the pages smiling, laughing, crying—remembering their "selves" and their stories. At our reading they recollected these memories yet again, and left their stories to be safeguarded by friends and loved ones, beyond the clutches of disease.

# THE FINANCIAL IMPACT OF ALZHEIMER'S

Bob Moos

As Bob Moos writes in this article for the *Seattle Times*, Alzheimer's disease is not just an emotional burden for caregivers but is also a financial burden. Medicare, which is a federal health insurance program designed to provide care for the elderly and disabled, does not cover the cost of a nursing home. This creates problems for many people who take on the financial responsibility of parents suffering from Alzheimer's disease. Moos emphasizes that because Alzheimer's destroys patients' reasoning abilities, it is particularly important for children to discuss financial decisions with their parents before the disease becomes severe. Bob Moos is a frequent contributor to the *Seattle Times*.

Sharon McIver spends a good part of her days stretching her 86-year-old mother's dollars as far as she can.

In the morning, the Dallas woman looks for sales on personal items her mother needs. After lunch, she makes a call to dispute an unusually large medical bill. And by evening, she has searched for the highest interest rate for her mother's bank certificates. "I feel as though I'm running two households," she explains. "It overwhelms me some days."

That's a common feeling among people who care for parents with Alzheimer's disease. An estimated 4.5 million Americans suffer from Alzheimer's, and an additional 4.8 million suffer from mild cognitive impairment, a condition that puts people at high risk of getting Alzheimer's.

Adult children like McIver shoulder many tasks as caregivers, but overseeing their parents' finances can be among the most difficult. The bills are staggering; they average $25,000 annually for home care and $50,000 per year for nursing homes. And financial resources often are limited; Medicare doesn't pay for long-term care. Alzheimer's patients with retirement nest eggs can exhaust their savings within several years.

Bob Moos, "Long-Term Caring: Planning Ahead Can Help Families Cope with Alzheimer's," *The Dallas Morning News*, August 16, 2004. Copyright © 2004 by *The Dallas Morning News*. Reproduced by permission.

After having her mother live with her, McIver moved her to an assisted-living center . . . "I just couldn't keep her with me anymore," she says. "Her dementia had become too severe." McIver's mother pays for her $118-a-day room with her savings and Social Security check. Yet as hard as McIver tries to stretch those dollars, she expects her mother to run out of money within three years. "After that," the daughter predicts, "her only option will be to go on Medicaid."

## Managing a Parent's Finances

Managing the money of aging parents is always a big responsibility, but it's especially true of Alzheimer's patients. Sons and daughters can't talk finances with parents whose mental faculties have dimmed. A person with Alzheimer's lives an average of eight years and sometimes as long as 20 after the onset of symptoms.

Geriatric care manager Kay Paggi of Richardson, Texas, has found that families often don't understand the financial implications when a parent is diagnosed with Alzheimer's. "Every week I hear from sons or daughters who think Medicare will cover their parents' long-term care," she says. "It's up to me to tell them the bad news. Medicare will cover hospital stays, but not extended care."

Financial advisers agree that families who think early about how to pay for an aging parent's care will have more options. "Money can be a touchy subject in any family—children are afraid to pry, and parents value their privacy," says Kevin Pittman of American Express Financial Advisers in Addison, Texas. "Still, I can't emphasize enough the importance of coming up with a financial plan as early as possible."

## Advice for Caregivers

Here are some points that experts say adult children should cover when they sit down with Mom or Dad to talk about their financial future and Alzheimer's care.

*Be tactful.*

Virginia Morris, author of "How to Care for Aging Parents," advises treading gently when you raise the issue of managing your parent's money. "Letting someone else take charge of your finances is a clear indication you're losing control of your life," she says. "It can be demeaning and hurt your self-esteem. Children must be mindful of that and always act respectfully."

*Put one person in charge.*

Elder-law attorney Janet Boyanton of DeSoto, Texas, says your parent should execute a document known as a durable power of attorney, which gives an individual of your parent's choosing the legal authority to act on his or her behalf until death. An attorney can help with the paperwork.

Boyanton advises against delay. If your parent becomes mentally incapacitated, you may need to go through the cumbersome process of gaining legal guardianship to manage financial affairs.

*Gather important documents and study them.*

Paggi says providing for your parent's care requires having a full understanding of the financial assets and liabilities. That includes checking and savings accounts, Social Security income, certificates of deposit, stocks and bonds, real-estate deeds, insurance policies and annuities, pension benefits, credit-card debts, home mortgages and loans, and so forth.

*Ask some basic questions. And consider consulting professionals.*

What are your parent's current financial needs and potential needs?

Morris says most families try to keep a parent with Alzheimer's at home as long as possible, hiring home-care aides to help. But for many, a nursing home eventually becomes necessary.

Is your parent able to pay for that care?

Calling on a financial adviser or geriatric-care manager may help in answering those questions and identifying community resources to defray the expenses.

*Think long and hard before cracking into your own nest egg.*

Paggi says she often has clients who spend their own retirement nest eggs on their parents' care. "There's no right or wrong choice; everyone needs to make the decision that works best for him," she says.

*Carefully evaluate nursing-home options.*

Experts say it's never too soon to start looking at nursing homes.

"Some have waiting lists, and you may need one for your parent before you think you do," Morris says. "And because Medicaid patients tend to have fewer choices, it's better to apply before your parent has exhausted his savings and your family still can pay."

*Know Medicaid's requirements.*

Families should become familiar with Medicaid's limits on the income and assets someone can have and still qualify for assistance, Boyanton says.

# CHAPTER 5

# PERSONAL STORIES ABOUT ALZHEIMER'S DISEASE

# THE AUGUSTE D. FILE: PORTRAIT OF THE FIRST ALZHEIMER'S PATIENT

Konrad Maurer and Ulrike Maurer

In their book *Alzheimer: The Life of a Physician and the Career of a Disease*, Konrad and Ulrike Maurer explain that the term *Alzheimer's Disease* was coined in 1910 by Emil Kraepelin, then director of a psychiatric clinic in Heidelberg. In 1901 Alois Alzheimer, a doctor and scientist who served as chief physician under Kraepelin, treated a patient named Auguste D., who exhibited symptoms of dementia normally found in patients much older than herself. Alzheimer drew links between her case and previous mental patients he had treated who exhibited shrinking of ganglial cells in the cerebral cortex of the brain, and he wondered if Auguste D. could have a similar condition. Thus, Alzheimer was the first to observe and note this new form of dementia. The authors point out that Alzheimer's belief that psychiatric disorders could be attributed to physical causes contradicted the Freudian ideas that were popular at the time. Auguste D. is called the first patient with Alzheimer's disease. Konrad Maurer is a neurologist, psychiatrist, psychotherapist, and director of the Psychiatric University Clinic in Frankfurt, Germany. His wife and coauthor Ulrike Maurer has converted the house in which Alois Alzheimer was born in Bavaria, Germany, into a museum and conference center.

"What is your name?"
 "Auguste."
"Family name?"
 "Auguste."
"What is your husband's name?"
 "I believe Auguste."
"Your husband?"
 "Oh, my husband . . ."
"Are you married?"

"To Auguste."

"Mrs. D.?"

"Yes, to Auguste D."

"How long have you been here?"

"Three weeks."

"What do I have in my hand?"

"A cigar."

"Right. And what is that?"

"A pencil."

"Thank you. And that?"

"A steel nib pen."

"Right again. What is that, Mrs. D.?"

"Your purse, doctor."

"Yes. Right. And that?"

"A book."

"And what is lying next to my notebook?"

"A bunch of keys."

"What does it consist of?"

"Individual keys."

Dr. Alzheimer, senior physician at the Asylum for the Insane and Epileptic in Frankfurt am Main, just wanted to get an overview of the new admittees from the previous day [November 25, 1901]. At first he only glanced at this file, but he simply could not put it down again: Auguste D., wife of a railroad clerk, born May 16, 1850. His assistant, Dr. Nitsche, had examined the patient the day before, between 10 and 11 o'clock. But Dr. Alzheimer sensed that there was something special about Auguste D. He decided to examine her himself. He did not yet know, on that gloomy November day, that he was making the most momentous decision of his life.

At midday Auguste D. had cauliflower and pork for lunch.

"What are you eating?"

"Spinach!"

She chewed the meat.

"What are you eating now?"

"First I eat the potatoes and then the horseradish."

Dr. Alzheimer showed her several objects. After a short time she no longer knew what she had been shown. In between she spoke repeatedly of "twins."

"Write 'Mrs. Auguste D.'"

She wrote "Mrs.," but she forgot the rest. She could write her full name if she was told each individual word. Instead of "Auguste," however, she wrote "Auguse."

She had trouble putting sentences together and showed signs of verbal perseveration.

Dr. Alzheimer was satisfied with the result of his first examination. He put her name and the date next to the sample of Auguste D.'s writing. He had never seen a patient forget her own name while writing. He described her behavior as an "amnesic writing disorder" and decided to continue his examination of Auguste D.

## November 28, 1901

Auguste D. was constantly fearful and at a loss. She said, over and over, "I won't let myself be cut," acted as if she were blind, walked about, groped the faces of other patients, and was struck by them in return. When asked what she was doing, she said, "I have to tidy up."

## November 29, 1901

She was placed in an isolation room, where she behaved quite calmly. When Alzheimer came in, she was again lying helplessly in bed.

"How are you?"

"It all comes to the same thing. So who carried me here?"

"Where are you?"

"At the moment; I have temporarily, as said, I don't have means. One has to just—I don't know myself—I don't know at all—oh, goodness gracious, what is it all?"

"What is your name?"

"Mrs. D. Auguste!"

"When were you born?"

"Eighteen hundred and . . ,"

"In which year were you born?"

"This year, no, past year."

"When were you born?"

"Eighteen hundred—I don't know."

"What did I ask you?"

"Oh, D. Auguste . . ."

"Do you have children?"

"Yes, a daughter."

"What is her name?"

"Thekla!"

"How old is she?"

"She is married in Berlin, Mrs. Wilke."

"Where does she live?"

"We live in Cassel!"

"Where does your daughter live?"

"Waldemarstrasse—no, different . . ."

"What is your husband's name?"

"I don't know . . ."

"What name does your husband have?"

"My husband isn't here right now."

"What is your husband's name?"

She answered all at once, quickly and as if she were waking up.

"August Wilhelm Karl; I don't know if I can state it just like that."

"What is your husband?"

"Clerk—I'm so mixed up—so mixed up—I can't."

"How long have you been here?"

"Two days probably . . ."

"Where are you?"

"That is probably Wilhelmshöhe."

"Where is your apartment?"

"Well, Frankfurt . . ."

"On which street?"

"Not Waldemarstrasse, so another, wait a moment; I am so very, so very . . ."

"Are you ill?"

"More downward, along the spine . . ."

"Do you know me?"

"I believe you have already treated me twice; no, excuse me, I can't so . . ."

"What year are we living in?"

"Eighteen hundred . . ."

"Which month?"

"Second month."

"What are the names of the months?"

Auguste D. rapidly recited the names of the months correctly.

"Which month is it now?"

"The eleventh."

"What is the eleventh month called?"

"So, the last—no, not the last . . ."

"Which?"

"I don't know so . . ."

"What color is snow?"

"White."

"Soot?"

"Black."

"The sky?"

"Blue."

"Grass?"

"Green."

"How many fingers do you have?"

"Five."

"Eyes?"

"Two."

"Legs?"

"Two."

"How many pfennigs make a mark?"

"A hundred."

"What does an egg cost?"

"Six or eight."

"Six or eight what?"

"Yes."

"Six or eight marks?"

"Yes, marks."

Dr. Alzheimer asked again about everyday things and asked her to do some arithmetic.

"What does a pound of meat cost?"

"Seventy."

"Seventy what?"

"I don't know . . ."

"A roll?"

"3 pfennigs."

"2 × 3?"

"6."

"9 × 7?"

"63."

"12 × 19?"

"27."

"6 × 8?"

"48."

"4 × 12?"

"48."

"If you buy six eggs at seven pfennigs each, what does that make?"

"Poaching."

"Which street do you live in?"

"I can't tell you that, I just have to wait a moment."

"What did I ask you?"

"So, that is Frankfurt."

"On which street do you live?"

"I can't tell you that, Waldemarstrasse—not, no."

"When did you get married?"

"I don't know that at the moment; indeed, the woman lives on the same corridor."

"Which woman?"

"The woman, where we live." Then she called loudly, "Mrs. Hensler, Mrs. Hensler, Mrs. Hensler. . . . She lives down here a level."

Again Alzheimer showed Auguste D. objects and had her read and write. She correctly named keys, a pencil, and a book.

"What have I shown you?"

"I don't know. . . . I don't know . . . so nervous, so nervous."

Dr. Alzheimer held up three fingers. "How many fingers am I holding up?"

"Three."

"Are you still nervous?"

"Yes."

"How many fingers did I show you?"

"Well, it's Frankfurt."

Dr. Alzheimer set out before Auguste D. a series of objects that she was meant to recognize by touch, with her eyes closed. Toothbrush, bread, roll, spoon, brush, glass, knife, fork, plate, purse, a mark piece, a cigar, and a key; she named them quickly and without difficulty. She described a metal cup as a milk pourer with a teaspoon. When she opened her eyes she said immediately, "A cup."

Her writing was the same as in previous days. Instead of "Mrs. Auguste D." she wrote "Mrs."; the rest she had forgotten and had to be told over and over again. As she wrote she said repeatedly, "I have, so to speak, lost myself."

In her reading she skipped between lines; some lines she read five times over. She appeared not to understand what she read; she stressed the words in unusual ways. Suddenly she spontaneously said the name "Quilling."

"Of course you know the Quillings?" During the rest of the examination she dwelled on the name "Quilling."

Dr. Alzheimer also performed a thorough physical examination. Apart from being underweight, she was physically normal. The apex beat was not palpable, the heart was not enlarged, and the pulmonic second sound was not audible.

At the center of his examination were the neurologic findings. The pupils reacted normally to incident light. The tongue, when stuck straight out, barely quivered but was extremely dry because of inadequate fluid intake. She wore dentures. She showed no disturbances in articulation. However, Auguste D. often interrupted herself while pronouncing words, as if she were at a loss or undecided as to whether what she was saying was correct.

During the examination she carried out all requests with rapid comprehension. She did not show signs of nervousness but did say suddenly, "A child just called! Is it there?"

"Do you often hear someone calling?"

"But you know Mrs. Quilling, of course!"

As she was to be taken from the isolation room to her bed she got worked up, screamed loudly, struggled, showed great fear, and called repeatedly, "I will not be cut! I will not let myself be cut!"

## November 30, 1901

Auguste D. often went into the main room, grabbed the faces of the other patients, and hit them. Because no one knew why she did this, she was isolated. Undeterred, Dr. Alzheimer continued his investigation.

"I don't feel like it and I don't have time."

"For what?"

"I would very much like to ask myself that."

"How are you?"

"It was quite good the last few days."

"Where are you?"

"Here and everywhere—here and now—you mustn't take offense."

"Where are you?"

"We will still live there."

"Where is your bed?"

"Where should it be?"

"How did you sleep last night?"

"Quite well."

"Where is your husband?"

"At the office; clerk, first class . . ."

"How old are you?"

"Fifty-seven years."

"Where do you live?"

"Waldemarstrasse . . ."

"Have you already eaten something today?"

"Yes, soup and various things."

"What are you doing now?"

"Yes, cleaning or something like that."

"Why haven't you gotten dressed?"

"I had things to do."

"How long have you been here?"

"You had written it down—fifty-seven."

"Fifty-seven what?"

She remains silent.

Auguste D. continued to behave strangely. She soon sent Alzheimer out of the room: "Please, you have no business being here."

Then she greeted him again as if he were a guest: "Do you want to take a seat? It's just that I still haven't had any time."

Later she pushed him out of the isolation room again and cried out loudly, like a child. Then she fell into a delirium in which she carried around her bedding, folded together the sheets and blanket, and sometimes shoved everything under the bed. She perspired from fear and repeatedly called "Karl" and "Thekla," the names of her husband and daughter.

Alzheimer asked her again, "What is your husband's name?"

"August!"

"Where are you?"

"At home." Sometimes she also said, "In the hospital."

Alzheimer had the impression that she no longer simply misunderstood but also was unable to do things. He instructed her, "Knit."

Auguste D. pulled all the needles out of her knitting and began to remove stitches from the middle. Alzheimer asked her what kind of furniture the commode was.

"That is my commode, please close the lid!"

As on the previous day, Auguste D. sat in bed helplessly, with a fearful expression. When Alzheimer entered the room she regarded him suspiciously. During the conversation she was tearful and reflected on her answers for a long time.

"You do not seem happy to see me at all," she said.

"Why?"

"I don't know. We didn't have debts or anything like that. I'm just nervous, you can't take offense at that."

"What is your name?"

"Mrs. Auguste D."

"What are you?"

"Mrs. Auguste D."

"How old are you?"

"Fifty-one."

"Where do you live?"

"Birthday? In Cassel."

"Where do you live?"

"Of course, you have already been to our house. Oh, I was only so nervous, please, please."

"Where do you live?"

"Mörfelder Landstrasse."

"Right! What year is it now?"

"One moment, I'm so nervous. So, how old am I? Fifty-one."

"What month is it?"

"The sixth—no—so, fifty-one. Yes, doctor, what have I done then, just tell me."

"What is today's date?"

"Fifty-one—no, I—am a bit nervous. Is that so bad, doctor? I don't know about anything."

"What day of the week is it today?"

"Sixty-five. Oh God, I used to be much better at sums."

"How long have you already been here?"

"Fifty-one."

"How long have you been here?"

"Oh, where do we live. Mörfelder Landstrasse."

"Which city are we in?"

"Cassel—here Cassel—no Frankfurt . . ."

"What kind of a building are you in?"

"That is . . . oh God. . . . Fifty-one . . . so fifty-one."

"What brought you here?"

"I actually don't know that—so fifty-one, 1851 . . ."

"What do you mean by that?"

"June fifty-one and . . ."

"Who are the people in your neighborhood?"

"Also in Mörfelder Landstrasse or . . . ?"

"Who are the people in your neighborhood?"

"Oh, I don't even know the people at all . . ."

"Where were you eight days ago?"

"Eight days ago? They say I can't remember."

"Where were you a month ago?"

"Yes, that I can't say."

"Where were you last Christmas?"

"Christmas."

"Where were you last Christmas?"

"Yes, I can't tell you that so precisely. . . . Fifty-one. . . . I still have to remember that first."

"Are you sad?"

"Oh always, mostly not; it happens that one sometimes has courage."

"Are you sick?"

"Oh, I can't actually say. I'm sorry enough when I . . . as I said . . . oh God . . ."

"Are you persecuted?"

"Oh no, by God no."

"Are you mocked?"

"Oh no, I definitely could not say that."

"Do you hear voices?"

"Yes, you've already said that to me."

"Do you hear voices?"

"Oh yes, so, humming perhaps."

"What hums?"

"Oh, it doesn't occur to me like that."

"Do you see shapes?"

"No, not at all."

"Who am I?"

"Oh, I already know."

"Who am I?"

In a whining tone Auguste D. answers, "I can't really say."

"Who am I?"

"Oh . . . oh . . ."

"Address me. What did you call me earlier? If you could just give me a bit of a hint."

"Doc . . . doctor."

"What am I?"

"Doctor."

Alzheimer was called to a patient who suddenly became agitated. An hour later he returned to Auguste D. Again he showed her various objects, which she named without touching them:

*Notebook:* "Book."

*Two-mark piece* [German currency]: "Two marks."

*Pencil:* "Pencil."

*Purse:* "Purse."

*Sleeve:* "Sleeve."

*Given Name:* Auguste
*Place of Birth:* Cassel
*Home:* Prussia
*Last Residence:* Frankfurt am Main, Mörfelder Landstrasse
*Year and Day of Birth:* May 16, 1850
*Marital Status:* Married
*Religious Confession:* Reformed
*Status or Profession:* Railway clerk's wife

The duration of illness Dr. Alzheimer entered himself: "half a year." To the question, "Are father and mother related to each other?" he answered, "No." There were nervous illnesses on her mother's side, and Auguste D. was not born out of wedlock. Next to the heading "Other Causes of Illness" he put "arteriosclerosis." The form of illness he labeled "arteriosclerotic brain atrophy" but marked the entry with a question mark. It also emerged from the admission sheet that Auguste D. had never been in legal trouble and had never been in a mental institution.

For the question, "Will the patient be cared for at own expense, first class, second class, third class, or at public expense third class?" Dr. Alzheimer underlined with his feather pen, "expense, third class." As form of illness, he wrote, "simple mental disorder."

On November 26, 1901, Nitsche had elicited a very thorough case history. According to his notes, Auguste D.'s mother had suffered from convulsions since menopause; however, during the attacks she did not drop objects that she held in her hands, nor did she lose consciousness. She had died of pneumonia at age sixty-four. The father had been healthy but died young, ostensibly from a "carbuncle on the neck." Auguste D.'s three siblings were in good health; no alcoholism or mental disorders were apparent in the family.

Auguste D.'s husband reported that his wife had always been healthy and had never had a serious illness. He said that they had been happily and harmoniously married since 1873. Auguste had had one daughter and had had no miscarriages. Her husband described his wife as constantly hard working and orderly; at most she was somewhat excitable and nervous but otherwise "rather amicable." She drank no alcohol, and there was no sexually transmitted disease in the family.

## Auguste D.'s Early Symptoms

According to the husband's statement, Auguste D. had been quite normal until March 1901. On March 18, 1901, she suddenly claimed that he had gone for a walk with a female neighbor. This completely groundless assertion was the first thing that struck him. From that moment on Auguste had been full of mistrust about him and this neighbor. Shortly thereafter the husband noted a decline in her memory. Two months later, in May, she made obvious mistakes in food preparation for the first time and became restless, wandering aimlessly through the apartment. She increasingly neglected her housework; her condition deteriorated more and more. She then claimed "constantly" that a carter, who often came into the house, wanted somehow to harm her.

Conversations she overheard she took to be about herself. No language or speech disorders, or even signs of paresis, had emerged. Recently she had spoken frequently of death and had become agitated, especially in the mornings, when she trembled, rang the neighbors' doorbells, and slammed doors shut. She was never violent. Shortly before being admitted to the hospital she had hidden all sorts of objects, throwing the house into disorder.

For Alzheimer it was easy to understand that under these circumstances her husband could no longer cope and, on November 25, 1901, he had brought his wife to the institution. The family doctor had noted in large script on the admittance note,

> Mrs. Auguste D., wife of the railway clerk Mr. Carl D., Mörfelder Landstrasse, has been suffering for a long time from weakness of memory, persecution mania, sleeplessness, restlessness. She is unable to perform any physical or mental work. Her condition (chronic brain paresis) needs treatment from the local mental institution.

## Dr. Alzheimer and Auguste D.

During the examination Alzheimer built a close and trusting relationship with Auguste D. His interest in her developed in part because of their shared hometown, Cassel. But Alzheimer also recognized very quickly that the case could prove to be of great scientific importance. He therefore arranged for a precise documentation of the course of the illness. He instructed the clinic photographer to take a number of pictures of Auguste D., including portrait photos.

Many photographs from June 1902 have been preserved. In one Auguste D. sits on a bench; in another she is in bed. On October 20, 1902, she was again photographed in bed.

In November 1902 a particularly impressive portrait emerged, a photo that almost a hundred years later, in 1997, was sent around the world. Auguste D. sits in her bed, turned to the side, with bent legs. She has full, long, dark brown hair; it hangs down both sides of her face in plaited strands. Her face is heavily wrinkled in the forehead and under the eyes; the folds alongside her nose are very prominent. Her face is thin, the exposed left ear rather large.

Auguste D. looks out blankly; she appears calm. Her well-groomed hands, with their strikingly long fingers, are folded over her knees. Auguste D. wears institutional clothing, a white nightshirt buttoned at the front.

Alzheimer developed the treatment plan himself. He prescribed baths for Auguste D. Alzheimer had done extensive work on the therapeutic value of warm and mild baths that extend over several hours, even days, and soothe agitated patients. A famous colleague, Emil Kraepelin, director of the Psychiatric Clinic in Heidelberg (and later Alzheimer's boss for a time), was also a champion of balneotherapy and climatology, which he had described in his 1896 textbook for students and doctors.

The initial treatment for insomnia was dietary. For patients with chronic illnesses and those with strong constitutions, extensive outdoor activity, exercise, and massage were prescribed, but strenuous physical exertions can cause sleeplessness in those who are easily excited or have recently become ill. For such patients, extended lukewarm baths with simultaneous cooling of the head and moist wrappings were preferred. Treating the head with weak electrical currents (galvanization) seemed appropriate to the physicians in some cases, as did hypnotic suggestion.

Often patients showed great improvement with the introduction of afternoon rest, light, early dinners, the avoidance of reading in the evening, abstention from tea and coffee, evening bowel evacuations, regular bedtimes, and extensive airing of the bedroom.

Alcohol was administered in mild doses. The doctors used sedatives only in emergencies—in cases of great fear or acute pain, for example—because it is difficult to reaccustom patients to natural sleep. In cases of extreme agitation refractory to other means, when rapid calming is necessary, chloroform was used.

In the treatment of Auguste D. and many other troubled patients, sedatives were very useful. Such patients were given 2 to 3 grams of chloral hydrate, a sedative that induced a longer-lasting, restful sleep. If the patient could not tolerate chloral hydrate, paraldehyde, an unpleasant-smelling and -tasting colorless liquid developed in 1883, could be administered. In small doses of 5 grams—which one can safely increase two- or threefold—it effects a long, deep, restful sleep, akin to natural sleep.

Amylene hydrate had certain advantages over paraldehyde; later sulphonal, tetronal, and somnol were used. The legendary Veronal (barbital), a barbituric acid preparation developed by Merck and Bayer, was still being tested on animals at this time and was not made available for patients for several years.

## The Last Months in the Asylum

In February 1902 Auguste D. suffered from constant restlessness and anxious confusion. She approached each day with such a negative attitude that examining her became impossible. Consequently, she spent the entire day, and often the evening, in the bath. At night she was usually put in an isolation room because she could not fall asleep in the main ward; she went to other patients' beds and woke them. In a private room, after a longer or shorter period of persistent wandering about, she fell asleep.

Alzheimer noted that she would never lie properly in her bed and did not use the bedding correctly. She covered herself with pillows and huddled on the feather quilt.

When she was calm during the day, she was placed in the open ward. During rounds, she approached the doctor with a helpless expression and used only empty phrases: "Oh, good day—so?" or "What would you like then?"

For a while she believed she was at home and receiving guests. Then she said, "My husband will be here shortly!" But she could not continue the scene and turned away, ran about aimlessly, and fiddled with her bedding. When the staff attempted to restrain her, she began to cry, moan, and voice her indignation, using meaningless words and expressions.

Alzheimer saw Auguste D. almost daily during his rounds and during the weekly rounds with the clinic director, Dr. Sioli. Her diet was good, but the long conversations he could conduct with her three months earlier were no longer possible.

Alzheimer's last entry in the files of Auguste D. dates from June 1902:

> Auguste D. continues to be hostile, screams, and lashes out when one wants to examine her. She also screams spontaneously, often for hours, so that she has to be kept in bed. As far as food is concerned, she no longer keeps to the regular mealtimes. A boil has formed on her back.

Alzheimer's last conversation with Auguste D. is well documented:
"Good day, Mrs. D."
"Oh, begone; I—cannot say—that."

Her agitation manifested itself in aimless wandering, purposeless activity, and especially loud wailing and screaming, which for several weeks appeared paroxysmal and lasted for several hours. Auguste D. appeared in a state of tremendous fear and called out, "Oh God—oh God—Heinrich!"

# Losing My Mind: A Firsthand Account of Alzheimer's

Thomas DeBaggio

In this excerpt from his book entitled *Losing My Mind: An Intimate Look at Life with Alzheimer's*, Thomas DeBaggio describes being diagnosed with Alzheimer's disease. He writes about his recognition of his early symptoms, the reactions of his friends and family to the diagnosis, and the lifestyle changes that Alzheimer's disease brings. Before being diagnosed with Alzheimer's, DeBaggio sold herbs and plants that he grew in his greenhouse and backyard. He has written three books on herbs, and he has also worked as a journalist.

My fifty-seventh birthday was pleasant and eventful and I began to adjust to middle age. I no longer noticed how small facial lines became wrinkles. I was active and happy. My son Francesco, home from California, joined Joyce and me in the family herb-growing business in Virginia. I was equipped with a thin body free of aches and pains. I looked forward to a life to rival my Midwestern grandmother's 104 years. I was buoyant and displayed, occasionally, the unbecoming arrogance of youth.

Then came a beautiful spring day later that year. It was the day after the tests were finished and the results reviewed. It was the day I was diagnosed with Alzheimer's. What time had hidden was now revealed. Genetic secrets, locked inside before my birth, were now in the open. I became a new member in the parade of horror created by Alzheimer's.

At first I viewed the diagnosis as a death sentence. Tears welled up in my eyes uncontrollably; spasms of depression grabbed me by the throat. I was nearer to death than I anticipated. A few days later I realized good might come of this. After forty years of pussyfooting with words, I finally had a story of hell to tell. . . .

## Failing Memory

After a short, mild winter, a vivid spring settled around us. The weather was tame and herbs filled a sunny patch next to the greenhouse. They were strong and vigorous now, especially the rosemaries, the thymes, the lavenders. Their scents perfumed the air when I brushed by them.

The sun warmed the earth steadily and it was possible to spade and plant a kitchen garden with early seed crops of succulent lettuce to sweeten and color our meals. It was a spring in which you could be happy and a little carefree. There was much the earth had to say and you could hear it if you stayed quiet and listened intently.

There was something else that spring and it was unnamable. As with all unknowns, it was unsettling and had nothing to do with the weather. It was not something that gentle rains, bright sunny days, and an optimistic outlook would cure. It was an anonymous presence, yet I could feel its uneasy cadence. My memory, which had been a sacred touchstone, was failing long before I expected. I was losing the ability to remember things important to me. I had difficulty recognizing the names of many of my plants, and even friends I saw infrequently. I was fifty-seven this year, and not eager to acknowledge that now I might be tied to a teetering mind that had begun a slow descent into silence.

A time or two I complained out loud that I could not remember things that the year before had been brightly colored and detailed. I brushed off those incidents as forgetfulness due to stress, and there was stress aplenty, as there had been always. Stress and worry were steady partners in my backyard farming, just as it was for the farmer in the great, flat Midwest with hundreds of acres of rich, black earth.

I made a living in my backyard for twenty-four years, growing and selling as many as 100,000 herb and vegetable plants from my greenhouse each spring. The entire operation, situated on a 5,000-square-foot lot, contained our family home and a 1,600-square-foot greenhouse. It marked me as a new breed of urban farmer who scorned grass and its wasteful, demanding cultivation. I made a living off the land by selling directly to gardeners the potted plants I started from seeds and rooted cuttings and grew carefully in the greenhouse.

It had always been tough outwitting nature. It was a struggle the mind and body accepted willingly by turning work into games. It was serious and enjoyable play for me, but it was also my livelihood. My family depended on my ability to tame nature and use my guileless skills to attract customers. From the beginning, my tangle with urban farming was a test of my strength and acumen against nature's unpredictability.

I was completing a doctor visit, a regimen that was new and uncertain to me, when my physician asked, "Is there anything you want to tell me?" He is a thoughtful, no-nonsense man with a sly sense of humor, and the question may have been the kind of thing he often says as he winds up a session with a patient.

"Yes, there is," I said. He said nothing and waited for my words. "I am having trouble remembering things that are basic to my work, things I have known and now can't remember."

There was silence while he looked at me. "I can give you a referral," he said quickly, careful not to confuse or cheapen my predicament with some offhand remark. "And I will have the nurse take additional blood samples for the doctor I am sending you to."

I made an appointment to have the blood drawn the next day at the clinic. After I dressed, one of the doctor's assistants gave me a piece of paper with another physician's name, address, and telephone number. I had never seen the name before and it meant nothing to me, but the address was a prestigious university hospital. The first four of many vials of blood yet to be drawn were taken the next day. . . .

## Alzheimer's Disease

In a test of my memory and ability to learn new things, I came out "severely impaired" according to my neuropsychological evaluation. Doctors say I am at the beginning of the disease's onslaught.

For a guy hardly sick in his life, this is a large, corrosive event. I am not alone. In a few years nearly half of those who reach eighty years old will have the disease, according to the Alzheimer's Association. I am not so lucky in another way. The disease is known to strike as early as thirty, but only a tiny minority falls in its clutches before the mid-sixties. At fifty-seven the disease has been active in me for longer than I know.

Instead of bringing this disease into sunshine where we can learn about it and do something, it has been too often hidden and misunderstood, closeted to protect the living from its frightening consequences. Alzheimer's does not have the drama of a heart attack or the thud of an automobile wreck.

Our understanding of the disease has been, until recently, held hostage by lack of knowledge. Now we know it was not undefined evil, profligate activity, or witchcraft causing the strange behavior created by the disease. We are close to understanding mechanisms triggering this ghostly malady. The disease, or its potential, appears to rest secretly inside us until its evil time arises and a languid torture begins. This is a disease probably not caused by something you did to your body. It is, most likely, a consequence of bad luck, subtle effects activated in the brain, and parents who carried corrupted genes.

The disease works slowly, destroying the mind, stealing life in a tedious, silent dance of death. Slowly the memory is impaired, and then you wander in a world without certainty and names. Yesterdays disappear, except those long ago. Eventually there is a descent into silence and a dependence on caretakers. Hands other than yours feed and bathe you. A cipher takes your place amid the tubes and tragedy. By the end, Alzheimer's leaves its victims silent, quivering in their flesh, awaiting the last rites. Some common illness often takes credit on the death certificate. . . .

This is an unfinished story of a man dying in slow motion. It is filled with graffiti, sorrow, frustration, and short bursts of anger. While the narrator suffers his internal spears, he tries to surround himself with memories in a wan attempt to make sense of his life and give meaning to its shallow substance before he expires. Although incomplete, the story is full of sadness and missed opportunity, a lonely tale of the human condition. Behind it is hope, the tortured luck of a last chance. . . .

## Medication

I am back from the drugstore with my packet of pills, prescription number 736631 from the CVS pharmacy, four blocks up the street. The pills have in them a pharmaceutical called Aricept, the trade name for donepezil HCl, the commonly prescribed medication for Alzheimer's at the time. The doctor told me the most common side effect is diarrhea. Boy, was he right.

I don't know whether to love these little round things or hate them. The pills are tiny and buff colored and on one side a "10" is stamped into it to designate it as a 10-milligram tablet and on the opposite side is the word Aricept. I started taking half of one of the tablets at bedtime. After five days, I was directed to take an entire tablet when I go to bed (later I began taking a second tablet before breakfast). Aricept was the second pharmaceutical developed for Alzheimer's and is now the most widely used medicine available, but at its best it can slow the destruction of brain cells temporarily.

The doctor also prescribed two over-the-counter medications to take daily: two vitamin E soft gels, each 1,000 international units, about 6,666 times more than the normally recommended dose, and a single Ibuprofen tablet. This combination of drug and vitamins is all medical science can do for me nearly 100 years after Alzheimer's was scientifically described. It seems a weak armada to defend against eager memory destroyers working in my brain. I am a citizen of a country that has sent mankind to the moon. It is sadly ironic but that is all medical science can do, when we spend billions to send men into outer space to look at rocks. . . .

## Symptoms

Suddenly I am surrounded by clutter. I look around my room. To the right of the computer is my desk. Floating on the desk are deep piles of paper, scattered envelopes, hastily scribbled notes. File folders full of papers almost cover the telephone, the two answering machines, and the fax. A white straight-sided coffee cup with blue lettering proclaiming Lawrence Welk Resort Village is stuffed with pens and a few pencils. A wire rack designed to hold envelopes bulges with bills. A bright-red *Webster's New World Dictionary*, second college edition, leans against the fax machine. The far corner is home for racks of file folders, my last attempt to bring order on the desktop, but they are holding piles of books and random sheets of paper. On top of the pile is one of my favorite books, *My Summer in the Garden*, by Charles Dudley Warner, published in 1874. Inside the front page is an inked inscription in clear script, "Abby Bassy, July 1, 1875." It was a gift from one of my customers years ago when I was smitten with Warner's garden writing.

On my left, there is better order but there are piles of books on top of books as well. I can hardly move around the floor. I have maintained, so far, a twelve-inch-wide path in which I can see the bare, dark wooden floor.

Elsewhere there are fall garden catalogs that will eventually be mailed, four pair of leather boots, two ready to be thrown away. There is also an assortment of large, open paper bags, empty and awaiting duty. The tops of the filing cabinets are covered with stray papers and books. Notes hang from the calendar attached to the white cabinets on the wall above my desk.

There is more of this mess that need not be cataloged. This is a tragedy for a man who was once tidy but it is a snapshot of a room that mirrors my brain, a jumble of words awaiting order with nowhere to go. Meaning is lost in a hurried moment, a word lost in confusion is never recovered. So it is that. Alzheimer's begins its conquest. . . .

## Visiting the Neurologist

The large rosemary bushes were awash with blossoms, splashy blue and subtle white. These were plants beautiful to observe in the spring when winter was mild, and as I inspected their small flowers and richly aromatic foliage, I was conscious of the plant's long history of medicinal use, an irony that was not lost on me. It was said that rosemary was for remembrance.

I called the neurologist to whom my family physician referred me and made an appointment. Several weeks later, I sat in his waiting room with people I knew had to be sicker than me. They were moaning and groaning in obvious pain and discomfort. There were people on crutches and in wheelchairs. The whole place was full of the infirm, the out-of-shape, the terribly ill, and they were all much older than me or in more pain.

In comparison I looked the picture of health and I wondered what they thought of me in their midst. If I had not been dressed so casually, they might have seen me as a salesman come to sell some ointment to the doctor. They must have wondered why I was there and that thought captured me. I was floating in a sea of doubt and I did not know what the outcome of this doctor visit would be, and that may have been the most troubling thing in my mind that afternoon.

I kept watching the clock. Waiting in a neurologist's office must be one of the modern world's more nefarious tortures. The technique of making a patient wait in a doctor's office is something that must be taught in medical school, a way to assure the patient the doctor is in charge and to telegraph how busy and important he is. It may also be a sign of how disorganized and overworked doctors are.

Finally a man in a white coat came into the waiting room and called my name. He had a hurried, brisk manner and he ushered me into a cramped, spare little office. He sat down at his desk and motioned me into a chair opposite him. The only humanizing thing in the room was a set of abstract watercolors on paper pinned to the wall next to the doctor. They turned out to be the work of his children.

The neurologist chatted for a while, outlining what he would do that day during the office visit. He began asking a few questions, gathering a wide array of personal information from me. As I talked he kept his head bowed over his notepad, writing with quick assurance, filling it with a dark, wiry scrawl.

"Mr. DeBaggio is a fifty-seven-year-old right-handed gentleman referred . . . for evaluation of memory loss," his notes say. "Patient has noted a problem with naming objects, onset about one-and-a-half years ago. Initially felt it was stress related but now is not sure. He is in the greenhouse-plant business and is having trouble remembering plants' names. Also however, may think of something that he needs in another room; may go into that room but then forgets why he went there. Believes this goes along with the naming problem."

The questioning continued for some time, covering my past medical history. The doctor learned what vitamins I took. Under family history/social history, he noted: "Married and has one son. Does not smoke. Drinks one-half glass of wine with dinner. Mother died of colon cancer and father died of heart disease."

The doctor stood up and walked over to the examining table and picked up a white hospital gown that lay there. He handed me the garment and asked me to undress and put on the gown. He left the room, saying he would return soon.

I changed into the hospital gown, a piece of clothing with which I was totally unfamiliar. It was style-less and not cut for warmth; the back was open and the room was chilled by air-conditioning. Garments like hospital gowns were undoubtedly designed to humble any person wearing them. I sat on the examining table, swinging my feet, waiting for him to return.

When the doctor returned, he asked me to stand and commenced an abbreviated physical exam. "Pleasant gentleman in no acute distress," his notes read. "Normal body habitus. Vital signs revealed a blood pressure of 140/80 with pulse of 70 and respiratory rate of 12. . . . Mental status resting revealed patient to be awake and alert."

Soon the type of questions changed direction and began to explore the workings of my mind in simple quick ways. Did I know where I was; what year was it; what month and day of the week? Then the doctor asked me to name the presidents of the United States, starting with the present officeholder and working backward; I got as far as Carter and he asked me to stop. "Simple and more complex calculations were intact," his notes say. "Could not reverse a five-letter word but could reverse a four-letter word. Short-term memory was three out of three objects immediately and one out of three objects after five minutes."

The most humiliating moment of the day occurred when I was asked to count backward from 100 by 7's. "Got serial sevens correctly back to 86," the neurologist noted, "subsequently said that he forgot what we were doing and then recalled on his own and then got serial sevens back to 58 correctly." That first tentative look at how my brain performed chilled me, no matter how much I made light of the methodology. Of course, neither of us knew for sure what caused the problems. The exercise illuminated the extent of how uncertain my memory had become and I found myself thinking I might be in deep mental trouble, but I dared not jump to conclusions quickly in a matter this serious.

There was an avoidance by the neurologist of the dreaded word "Alzheimer's" but it was clearly one of the options being considered. It was necessary, however, to search for other causes that might also produce similar conditions and he told me his secretary would get in touch with me to set up appointments with other specialists.

Later, when I read a copy of his notes, I came across what the neurologist's initial conclusion had been. It was chilling. From just a few simple tests, the neurologist wrote the impression: "Mild dementia versus age-related memory loss plus anxiety. Suspect the former, rule out the latter. Rule out treatable cause."

Dementia is a word used by specialists in this field to define loss or impairment of mental powers from organic causes, often Alzheimer's. It was clear that the doctor detected from his examination the familiar opening stages of Alzheimer's, but he wanted to rule out other causes. Somehow I remained optimistic.

Before I left the neurologist, he wrote an order for more blood to be drawn from me and I went downstairs and waited a few minutes. I was escorted into a small room and a nurse took four or five additional vials of blood.

Within a few days, the doctor's efficient secretary called to tell me she had made a series of appointments for me with specialists who met the approval of my HMO and I prepared for my round of testing. . . .

## Family

I have talked to my son Francesco often about what I am going through. I realized the other day my openness may be a large problem for him. He must be troubled by what he sees happening to me, the slow march of disease that sends me stuttering for words. Yet he is quiet about it, watching me carefully, and searching inside himself for some early sign that my Alzheimer's was passed on to him.

When I shut my eyes at night, before I go to sleep, I am given what I imagine is a tour of my brain. Pictures of the day pass before my closed eyes and I am treated to an abstract phantasmagoria: bouncy colored lights, mountains in fantastic colors, pictures that resemble the landscape of the moon seen from a slow-moving vehicle. It is as if a television camera tuned in my brain to show me sights streaking across an inner sky. It is a moving canvas I see on which a painter delights in mixing colors and then throws them into my sleepy mind. Some nights the visual pyrotechnics are so strong it is difficult to get to sleep, something that has never happened to me before. Eventually the random shapes begin to take form and recognizable objects and scenes appear. I detect a story but then I may be asleep, or am I? . . .

Joyce is much more than my wife, and always has been. Primarily she is a printmaker. As an artist, she is a trained observer; minutia sometimes appears to be her first love. She scrutinizes me now more than she did several years ago.

At times she is my translator and word finder when my mind slinks away from the job it was hired to do. At this stage in the disease, life is normal; only in subtle ways am I different than I was a few years ago. Joyce and Francesco pick up these subtleties in a way that even friends might not. What is happening is hidden inside my brain and it will take time for it to be fully noticed.

Joyce grew up in a family of secrets and few words. She was not scared by her father's or mother's ways, but stripping to her soul in public is not her style. I am in the early stages of the disease and with few minor exceptions our lives are not much different than they were fifteen years ago. I drive the car, prepare my share of suppers, go grocery shopping, and do chores, but it would be inaccurate to say that Alzheimer's has not touched us. . . .

A new world greets me every morning now. I will never see myself or the world the same way. I must cling to optimism and avoid depression, but today I am so shattered I can hardly hold a word, phrase, or sentence long enough to acknowledge it and put it on paper. It is as if I received a death sentence and I have to begin a circumscribed life in a prison of fear. I see myself differently, almost as if a death ray penetrated me. I look in a mirror and discover I am crying. . . .

I am still stunned by Joyce's reaction to my diagnosis. Though it is no wonder, she sprang at the doctor verbally. She heard a stranger abruptly inform her to prepare for an end to her life with me, a physically agonizing termination and brutally drawn out. Lacking was an explanation of his conclusions, what was known and what could be done. Instead, fires of miscommunication burned out of control. Sorrow without tears is an empty emotion. A scream is worth a thousand words sometimes.

Joyce was brave with echoes of her days on picket lines, and anger filled her body with consternation. She erupted with swinging questions. She wanted explanations, not statements that the doctor didn't know the person who had conducted the tests. It wasn't that she didn't believe the tests, she wanted knowledge to give her understanding. She was not going to let this M.D. off the hook with a smile and a prescription. I watched as she swirled in early bereavement and lashed out for answers and cures were the province of darkness. . . .

## Coping

Friends often ask me unanswerable questions after I tell them of the Alzheimer's diagnosis. "Are you certain of the diagnosis?" "It can't be true. You look so healthy; the doctors have made a mistake."

It does look and feel like Alzheimer's in its beginning stages, but it is not something I have had before; this is no simple memory loss that rest and recreation improves. Does it matter what is causing my memory to fail me? Probably not. If all the doctors are wrong, it won't make any difference. I am going to live as long as I can; that has always been my goal. I am also a realist and I have begun to adjust my life so each day has a structure to it, and a purpose: to enjoy every minute I can and to focus on the work I love with herb plants, and with words. I want to write the truest sentences I can in the hope my words give others the sense of struggle and joy I feel. . . .

I do not want to succumb to this illness but I am powerless in its clutches. Words come when I sit down to write, but they dance away seductively, and meaning and substance disappear quickly. Of course, this is not new; such things happen many times, but before they were retrievable and now they are not.

# Nancy and Ronald Reagan Face Alzheimer's

Anne Edwards

In this excerpt from her biography *The Reagans: Portrait of a Marriage*, Anne Edwards describes Ronald Reagan's diagnosis of and subsequent descent into Alzheimer's disease. In 1989, the last year of his second term as president, doctors removed fluid from Reagan's brain discovered during an examination following an accident in which Reagan was thrown from his horse. Nancy Reagan would later blame that accident for contributing to the development of his Alzheimer's disease, though as of this writing there is no conclusive evidence that a single trauma to the head is a cause of Alzheimer's. However, after leaving office, Ronald Reagan became increasingly forgetful, confused, and disoriented. In November 1994, he announced his Alzheimer's disease in an open letter to the nation.

Edwards emphasizes Nancy Reagan's devotion and care for her husband as he loses his cognitive abilities. The author also describes how Nancy Reagan's daughters rallied to support her as the former president became more and more sick. Ronald Reagan died of Alzeihmer's on June 5, 2004.

Anne Edwards is the author of many biographies about celebrities, including Katherine Hepburn and Maria Callas.

The Reagans were looking forward to spending the Fourth of July and Nancy's birthday on July sixth [1989] with their old friends Bill and Betty Wilson at their magnificent ranch in the Mexican state of Sonora (Bill Wilson had served under Reagan as the first U.S. ambassador to the Vatican and had also been responsible for finding Rancho del Cielo for the Reagans). The morning of July fourth was a spectacular day. The sun was glittering, the air so clear, the sky so blue, that it seemed as though you could see forever. The Wilsons' ranch included some of the most beautiful country in Sonora and riding paths that allowed fantastic views. Two Secret Service men came with them, but as Reagan and Wilson were the superior equestrians, they led the group. Reagan was on a spirited horse. That had never bothered him, but it did mean that horse and rider were not yet well acquainted.

They were proceeding down a rocky, downhill slope, when there was a rustle underfoot, most probably a snake, and Reagan's horse bucked wildly several times, his rider holding on tenaciously before being thrown off the animal onto the hard, graveled earth, his head hitting a rock. When his two Secret Service bodyguards and Bill Wilson reached him a split second later, he was stunned. He tried to sit up while the others restrained him.

One of the bodyguards used his cell phone to get assistance and within ten minutes the whir of a helicopter could be heard overhead. Reagan was flown, with Nancy, to Raymond W. Bliss Army Community Hospital at Ft. Huachuca, Arizona, where after X-raying and examining him, the doctors assured him that he had sustained bruises and a minor concussion but no serious injuries. "Well, honey," he grinned at Nancy, "I guess I had my own private rodeo." At his insistence they were flown back to the Wilsons' ranch by helicopter that same afternoon, accompanied by Capt. Juan Lopez, a U.S. Army doctor and the hospital's chief nurse, Lt. Col. Paul Farineau. The next day, against their advice and Nancy's admonitions, he was back up in the saddle. "There is nothing better for the insides of a man than the outsides of a horse," he was fond of saying.

In all the years of their marriage, Nancy had worried about many things but never Ronnie's handling of a horse. She had been badly frightened by the accident. She noticed small lapses of memory from that time on, and always blamed the fall from the horse as being the major cause of the disease that would eventually assail him as it had Nelle [Ronald Reagan's mother], and only recently, Neil [Ronald Reagan's brother], who no longer recognized his younger brother. A small blood clot had shown up when Reagan was reexamined in Los Angeles shortly after his return from Mexico, but it dissolved without surgery within a week.

The Reagans always had annual examinations at the Mayo Clinic in Rochester, Minnesota, and both were scheduled on September 7 for their 1989 checkup. Nancy was found to be in good health, but a CAT scan (not usually included in a general examination but done because of the earlier blood clot) located fluid on the right side of Reagan's brain (a condition that is known as a chronic subdural hematoma). A relatively simple procedure was ordered, which involved drilling a hole in the right side of the head and draining the fluid. Reagan entered St. Mary's Hospital in Rochester, where, on September 9, he underwent an hour-long surgery performed by a team of Mayo Clinic doctors. They removed the fluid on his brain.

He remained at St. Mary's, Nancy at his side, until September 16, his natural good humor seeming untouched as he joked about "the GI haircut" the doctors had given him. On Friday the fifteenth, he was visited by the maverick Soviet Communist Boris Yeltsin. Through interpreters the two men exchanged jokes. One example of Yeltsin's humor is a story he told about his first encounter with the Statue of Liberty: "I flew around it in a helicopter and I felt much freer, so I asked the pilot to fly around it again and then I felt completely free.". . .

## Symptoms of Alzheimer's

Reagan believed that retirement was for other people, not for him. He dressed impeccably every morning, and was driven to his spacious office suite, spending several hours at his desk talking to a few select people and conducting the usual rituals of a former president. Hundreds of letters arrived every week requiring an answer, including endless requests for him to make a public appearance. He accepted very few. A former secretary claims that at least until the end of 1992, when she left his employ, Reagan closely followed domestic and foreign affairs and kept in touch with former presidents Ford and Carter and the incumbent president, George H. W. Bush. (She could not recall that he ever spoke directly with Bush's successor, Bill Clinton.)

Sometime toward the end of 1993 Nancy became alarmed after they had flown to Chicago, where Reagan was to give a speech. Once they had been driven to their hotel and led into their suite, he turned to her and said, "I'm afraid I don't know where I am."

Marion Jorgensen, at whose home he had always spent election eves, recalled an evening about this same time when he came into her living room with Nancy and suddenly a puzzled look clouded his face as he glanced at his hostess and then out the window, "This place is familiar to me," he said. "I know I've been here before." And then came a dinner for Mrs. [Margaret] Thatcher [former prime minister of Great Britain] where he repeated a paragraph in his honoring speech to her without realizing he had done so.

The times he seemed confused, not sure of where he was became more frequent. He would enter a room purposefully and then pause, a look of some bewilderment in his puzzled eyes. Long moments could pass with him in this state, and often he needed assistance to return to his desk. "Who are you?" he asked a secretary who had been with him for years.

Nancy's fear mounted. Ronnie had always had two distinct sides to his personality. On the one hand he was gregarious, enjoying the company of a few or of many; stories, theories, commentary with great enthusiasm, often shot with a touch of down-home humor. He could also be a loner, withdrawn. His daughter Patti recalls that shortly before he was elected president she looked over at him "standing in the middle of a crowd, alone. People were around him but no one was talking to him. . . . It was one of those cocktail party moments that usually goes [sic] unnoticed. Except I noticed, and I remembered it."

Early in their relationship Nancy had accepted Ronnie's moments of separateness. She understood, when others did not, that he was an extraordinary man. But he was never hesitant in showing her how much he loved her or in telling her and anyone who would listen how indispensable she was to his life. And he never was shy about expressing his love for her in public by holding her hand, or placing his large, well-muscled arm around her narrow, delicate shoulders. "Powder down your lipstick," he once telegraphed when he was out barnstorming for GE. He was on his way home and could not wait to kiss her. She had received from him well over a hundred letters, notes, telegrams, and cards, all declaring his great love for her. The presidency and the passing years had not stopped their flow, but his growing confusion had. No longer could Nancy attribute his lapses to ordinary forgetfulness. She now refused to leave his side except for those times when he was in his office and surrounded by loyal and protective staff.

## Accepting the Diagnosis

Still, it was difficult for her to admit that anything deeply serious was taking place. He retained his social skills. He seemed to be willing himself to hang on to some semblance of the normal. They saw their old, trusted friends—Betsy Bloomingdale, the Deutsches, the Wicks, the Jorgensens, and the Annenbergs, among numerous others. They visited people's homes, or their friends came to theirs. Nancy became almost custodial, not wanting Ronnie to be placed in any situation that could lead to public embarrassment. By the summer of 1994 his lapses, his moments of confusion, worsened, and he submitted to medical tests and a brain scan at the Mayo Clinic. The dreaded diagnosis of Alzheimer's disease was made. At this time he was cognizant enough—his lapses interspersed with reasonably lucid intervals—to understand what he had and what it meant.

"His courage was outstanding," one close friend says, "but so was Nancy's."

He and Nancy discussed what he should do. She pledged that she would, as always, remain by his side. Theirs was an unalterable love. Determined to make something good of this tragic news, Reagan decided to tell the American people the truth, so that perhaps he could take some of the stigma off the disease. He sat down and began writing a draft the way he had always begun his speeches. He wrote it at his desk in the comfortable library of the Bel Air house, Nancy seated across from him as he moved his pen with a somewhat shaky hand. Most of his speeches had been written in this manner, marked with hen scratches as he edited his first thoughts. This letter took longer than usual, but the first draft of his last communication to the American people has only one correction—a line through the letter *I* in the middle of a sentence where he might have forgotten, for a moment, what he wanted to say. The draft is in his distinct hand.

On November 5, 1994, he bade the country his moving, brave goodbye, ending with: "I intend to live the remainder of the years God gives me on this earth doing the things I have always done. I will continue to share life's journey with my beloved Nancy and my family. . . . Unfortunately, as Alzheimer's Disease progresses, the family often bears a heavy burden. I only wish there was some way I could spare Nancy from this painful experience. When the time comes I am confident that with your help she will face it with faith and courage. . . ."

Nancy was once quoted as saying about her relationship with the media, "If it rains, I get blamed for it." Now they rallied to her side. It helped—but only a little bit. Her concentration was on how to make Ronnie's life meaningful in view of his inevitable decline and on how to protect him and to preserve his dignity.

## Life After the Diagnosis

He continued with his daily trips to his office. There was a pretense that things were as they had always been, at least in the first years after the end of his administration. But he remained behind closed doors while "business as usual" was being conducted by his staff. Only a few trusted colleagues were allowed to visit him. Before they arrived, Nancy ordered the staff to make sure that framed photographs of that person with Reagan or of events in which the guest had participated be placed in strategic positions on tables and shelves so as to catch his eyed as he ushered the guest into his private study. Before the visitor's arrival, Nancy (or a secretary on her orders) would walk Ronnie around the room looking at the photographs to refresh whatever residual memories existed: "This is when he visited us at the ranch." "Here you both are on the plane during the second presidential campaign." He would then repeat to his guest what he had just been told when he or she arrived moments later and he took them on a tour through his office. By 1998 his condition had so deteriorated that Nancy decided the office had to be closed and that Ronnie should be seen only by close family members. She called some of his oldest associates, like Michael Deaver, who for three decades had been his loyal aide and longtime family friend, to come and say goodbye.

When Deaver entered, Reagan "was sitting at his desk reading a large book. . . . he didn't look up," Deaver recalled. "He looked pretty good, I thought. Blue suit, French cuffs—for a man then in his late eighties, he was well turned-out." Deaver realized that he could stand there all day without Reagan taking notice of him and that he would "have to take charge if there was going to be any conversation."

"Hi," Deaver blurted, moving toward the desk.

After an awkward pause, Reagan looked up, his gaze "questioning and unrecognizing."

"Yes," he said, his voice polite. Then he returned his attention to the open book.

"Whatcha reading?" Deaver asked.

"A horse book," he replied.

Deaver glanced over at what Reagan was holding in his hands. "It was a picture book about Traveller, General Robert E. Lee's horse. I felt like crying," he recalled. Reagan had no memory of who Deaver was or how close the two once had been, for a good part seeing each other daily, over a span of thirty years.

Nancy kept her fears mostly to herself, although she spoke of them to confidants Betsy Bloomingdale and Merv Griffin, "and if anyone knew her true feelings it was them." She converted the house into a home where Ronnie could receive round-the-clock care and yet not be isolated from her. She was with him on a daily basis and supervised his mealtimes whenever possible. She talked to him about the family and all that was going on, despite the knowledge that little of what she said made sense to him. (This was in the late 1990s.) According to one staff member, "Mrs. Reagan was remarkable. She kissed the president's forehead, gently pushed his hair back from it, patted his hand and smiled—oh, my, how she smiled at him. It broke your heart. But at some point he would look at her and smile back. I don't believe she ever did, or ever could, let go of the idea that he knew who she was. Whether he did or not, he was aware that she was someone who cared for him, and he responded to that."

During the last year of his cognition, Reagan's faith in God never appeared to waver. He was never known to have asked why God could have allowed this to happen to him, nor to display anger toward Him. Like Nelle, he accepted God's will. This disease, after all, was not man's doing. Nancy was no martyr. She was frustrated at times. Frightened at others. She grieved for what their life once had been. But Ronnie was in a safe place. He was not in pain, nor was he aware of what he had lost. For Nancy, the hardest thing to accept was that for Ronnie the past had slipped away. He no longer remembered that he had been the president of the United States, he no longer recognized his children, or even recalled their existence, nor knew that he had shared with Nancy a splendid love. These were the things that were almost unbearable. But for as long as she lived, she would become his memory.

## The Family Copes

She took over the supervision of his correspondence (which still came in at a tremendous rate), as well as her own, along with all decisions that had to be made on their personal affairs and on the running of their household. She kept up with the newest medications for Alzheimer's and had frequent consultations with his doctors and their accountant. As always, the large expenditures for the house and care were of great concern to her. But in 1998 she sold Rancho del Cielo for a reported $6 million to the Young America's Foundation, a conservative group with its main offices in Santa Barbara, for use as a conference center. When not dealing with his care or spending time with Ronnie, Nancy threw herself into numerous charitable projects, into working with the staff at the Ronald Reagan Presidential Library, into the compilation of a book composed of Ronnie's love letters to her through the years (published as *I Love You, Ronnie*), and in 2002 she privately lobbied support for stem-cell research in hopes that the results of such work could eventually help early victims of Alzheimer's disease.

With the passage of the years, Nancy's greatest fear had been of a time when she would have to face life without Ronnie. Now she was fearful of how she would cope while he was alive. She wanted, above all, to maintain for him his dignity, to preserve in the minds of the people of the world an image of him conveying strength and purpose, the leader of the free world. Her job, as she saw it, was to protect his image as vigilantly as she would protect the man, especially now that he could not look after himself.

Her father's decline brought Patti close, for the first time in years, to her mother. Nancy managed to put aside her ill-feelings regarding Patti's literary excursions into their family history. "I need her now, more than ever," Nancy was known to have said. With her father slipping away from her, Patti was, as she would say, shocked as to "how the years could have gone by so fast, how we [her father and herself] could have been so reckless with time, with words, with our hearts." One day, during a visit when he no longer recognized her, she took his hand in hers and remembered "how his hands had once chopped firewood and assembled Christmas toys for [Ron and herself]. When, I wondered, did his fingers lose their calluses, when did they become so delicate?" Patti would never be able to have that reconciliatory confrontation with her father, the exchange that she always had hoped would lead to his understanding her. Now she wished that she had better understood him, but this realization came too late. She would not let this happen with her mother.

With Nancy so involved with his care, Maureen took on the task of being her father's spokesperson, appearing at various venues where he was to be honored in some way. One of her favorite journeys was to Dixon, where, she said, her "father's heart has always been . . . and it always will be." He had often told her stories of growing up in what he called "the greatest town in America." Dixon, with the help of Congress, was setting up the house on Hennepin Street where he had lived from 1924 to 1928 as a national historic site. The streets he walked on his way to school and church were named the Ronald Reagan Trail. A statue of him was placed in Lowell Park. At the dedication of all these tributes to the humble hometown boy who had become president, Maureen would appear, flashing her winning Reagan smile, filled with exuberance and tales about the father whom she idolized, never a bad word said, never a mention of his years of inattention.

Maureen and Dennis, who were childless, had adopted Rita, a young girl of color, toward the end of Reagan's presidency, and he had taken much pleasure in teaching her how to swim. By the late nineteen-nineties Rita was in her teens and accompanied her mother to Dixon. "My grandfather wasn't always a 'honcho,'" Rita commented to a group of teenagers at Ronald W. Reagan Middle School in Dixon. "He started out as a guy, just like us." The Reagans had three grandchildren—Cameron and Ashley Reagan and Rita Revell—but none of them carried the genes of Nancy or Ronald Reagan.

Ronald Reagan celebrated his eighty-sixth birthday, February 6, 1997, with Nancy, blew out a candle on his favorite chocolate cake, and was still sharp enough to make a comment (possibly scripted for him) that this was "the forty-seventh anniversary of my thirty-ninth birthday." Until 1999 he managed to play a few supervised holes of golf once or twice a week. The time finally came when he had to be moved to the separate suite that adjoined the master bedroom that Nancy had prepared for him. After a fall in 2001, when he broke his hip, Nancy hired three shifts of nurses to care for him upon her return home from the hospital, his hip now pinned. She complained to friends about the financial burden and about the inequitable pension given presidents upon their retirement, but never about the physical and emotional difficulties of her life.

Perhaps the one kind thing his memory loss spared Reagan was the grief when Maureen died in August 2001 of a melanoma that had spread to the bone. Through the years Mermie had become the child to whom he was the closest.

## Nancy After Ronald

Nancy's aura had done a complete about-face. Now she was viewed with grave respect by the media. After the death of Jackie Kennedy Onassis, Nancy was accorded the status of the brave widow, without actually being widowed. Her beloved other had lived on year after year after year, the once strapping physique that had made her feel so feminine now frail; the vibrant voice that had so stirred the patriotic instincts of his countrymen and women a faint whisper; his past, the most glorious a man born in the United States could experience—the humble boy rising to the presidency—lost to him. Nancy would sit by his bed and talk to him. Although he did not comprehend what she was saying, nor was Nancy certain he actually knew who she was, her voice did touch something that memory had once lighted, and he seemed calmed, reassured. He would smile, and the smile transformed his pale, almost skeletal face so that the man he once was became fleetingly apparent again.

Nancy published her book of his love letters in 2001 to show the world just how much she had meant to him. She christened an aircraft carrier, the USS *Ronald Reagan*, which was twenty stories high and could go twenty years without refueling its nuclear engines, a use of nuclear power that she knew Reagan would have heartily approved. She accepted the nation's highest honor, the Congressional Gold Medal, in both their names. Her past iniquities were not forgotten, but they paled under the bright, steady light of her devotion. She stood for loyalty in the extreme and symbolized a love that satisfied the weepiest sentimentalist.

The Reagan presidency was also being rethought by the public and political pundits. He had earned a reverence from the nation's citizens that was akin to worship. He had seen his country as being confronted by evil, "and the Communist states as simply the latest enemy that needed to be defeated rather than accommodated." Whether he was largely responsible for the dismantling of the Berlin Wall and the collapse of the Soviet state remains for history to decide. But he had made his mark. He would be long remembered and held in obeisance by many (and perhaps in disfavor by many as well). And while you cannot compare the Reagans' marriage to those of John and Abigail Adams, James and Dolley Madison, or Franklin and Eleanor Roosevelt, because each couple has its own dynamics, throughout history they will always be thought of as a team. Could Nancy ever have wished for more?

# ORGANIZATIONS TO CONTACT

The editors have compiled the following list of organizations concerned with the issues debated in this book. Descriptions are derived from materials provided by the organizations. All have publications or information available for interested readers. The list was compiled on the date of publication of the present volume; names, addresses, phone and fax numbers, and e-mail/Internet addresses may change. Be aware that many organizations take several weeks or longer to respond to inquiries, so allow as much time as possible.

**AARP**
601 E St. NW, Washington, DC 20049
(888) 687-2277
Web site: www.aarp.org

AARP, formerly known as the American Association of Retired Persons, is a nonpartisan association that seeks to improve the aging experience for all Americans. It is the nation's largest organization of midlife and older persons, with more than 30 million members. AARP publishes the magazine *Modern Maturity* and the newsletter *AARP Bulletin*. Links to current news on Alzheimer's disease can be found on its Web site.

**Administration on Aging (AOA)**
Washington, DC 20201
(202) 619-0724
Web site: www.aoa.dhhs.gov

The Administration on Aging works to protect the rights of the elderly, prevent crime and violence against older persons, and investigate health care fraud. AOA's Web site provides information on issues of aging, such as age discrimination, elder abuse, and Alzheimer's disease, as well as links to other useful resources.

**Alzheimer's Association**
225 N. Michigan Ave., 17th Fl., Chicago, IL 60601-7633
(800) 272-3900 • fax: (312) 335-1110
Web site: www.alz.org

The Alzheimer's Association's mission is to find a cure for Alzheimer's disease as well as to provide information and support to Alzheimer's patients and their families and caregivers. Its Web site provides information on current theories, research, and news about Alzheimer's. The site also provides glossaries and fact sheets.

**Alzheimer's Disease Aging and Referral Center**
PO Box 8250, Silver Spring, MD 20907-8250
(800) 438-4380
Web site: www.alzheimers.org

The Alzheimer's Disease Aging and Referral Center provides a rich source of information on Alzheimer's disease, including treatment and caregiving resources. The organization publishes a quarterly newsletter that is available on its Web site.

### Alzheimer's Disease Research Center
Johns Hopkins Medical Institute
Johns Hopkins University
Department of Pathology, Ross 558, 720 Rutland Ave., Baltimore, MD 21205
(410) 502-5164 • fax: (410) 955-9777
e-mail: delmael@jhmi.edu • Web site: www.alzresearch.org

The Alzheimer's Disease Research Center's main goal is to find and create effective treatments for Alzheimer's disease. The Web site offers information about the many research projects that scientists at this center are performing toward the goal of finding more effective treatments.

### American Geriatrics Society (AGS)
Empire State Bldg., 350 Fifth Ave., Suite 801, New York, NY 10118
(212) 308-1414 • fax: (212) 832-8646
e-mail: info@americangeriatrics.org • Web site: www.americangeriatrics.org

The American Geriatrics Society is a professional organization of health care providers that aims to improve the health and well-being of all older adults. AGS helps shape attitudes, policies, and practices regarding health care for older people. The society's publications include the book *The American Geriatrics Society's Complete Guide to Aging and Health*, the periodicals *Journal of the American Geriatrics Society*, *Annals of Long-Term Care: Clinical Care and Aging*, and the *AGS Newsletter*.

### American Health Assistance Foundation
22512 Gateway Center Dr., Clarksburg, MD 20871
(800) 437-2423 • fax: 301-258-9454
Web site: www.ahaf.org

The American Health Assistance Foundation supports research on Alzheimer's disease and other disorders. It also has a public education program, and it assists families by relieving some of the financial burden that Alzheimer's can cause.

### American Health Care Association (AHCA)
1201 L St. NW, Washington, DC 20005
(202) 842-4444 • fax: (202) 842-3860
Web site: www.ahca.org

The American Health Care Association is a federation of fifty state health organizations that represent nearly twelve thousand assisted living, nursing facility, and subacute care providers. AHCA provides information and education that help enhance quality care. It publishes the monthly magazine *Provider* and the monthly newsletter *AHCA Notes*.

### American Society on Aging
833 Market St., Suite 511, San Francisco, CA 94103
(800) 537-9728 • fax: (415) 974-0300
e-mail: info@asaging.org • Web site: www.asaging.org

The American Society on Aging is an organization of health care and social service professionals, researchers, educators, businesspersons, senior citizens, and policy makers that is concerned with all aspects of aging. It works to enhance the well-being of older individuals. Its publications include the bimonthly newspaper *Aging Today* and the quarterly journal *Generations*.

## Cato Institute

1000 Massachusetts Ave. NW, Washington, DC 20001-5403
(202) 842-0200 • fax: (202) 842-3490
Web site: www.cato.org

The Cato Institute is a libertarian public policy research foundation dedicated to limiting the control of government and protecting individual liberties. The institute provides articles and studies about Alzheimer's disease on its Web site. The Cato Institute publishes the magazines *Regulation* and *Cato Journal*.

## International Federation on Ageing (IFA)

425 Viger Ave. West, Suite 520, Montreal, Quebec H2Z 1X2 Canada
(514) 396-3358 • fax: (514) 396-3378
e-mail: ifa@citenet.net • Web site: www.ifa-fiv.org

The International Federation on Ageing is a private nonprofit organization that brings together over 150 associations that represent or serve older persons in fifty-four nations. IFA is committed to ensuring the dignity and empowerment of older persons. It publishes the quarterly journal *Ageing International* and the monthly newsletter *Intercom*.

## National Association for Home Care (NAHC)

228 Seventh St. SE, Washington, DC 20003
(202) 547-7424 • fax: (202) 547-3540
Web site: www.nahc.org

The National Association for Home Care believes that Americans should receive health care and social services in their own homes. It represents home care agencies, hospices, and home care aide organizations. NAHC publishes the quarterly newspaper *Homecare News* and the monthly magazine *Caring*.

## National Citizens' Coalition for Nursing Home Reform (NCCNHR)

1424 Sixteenth St. NW, Suite 202, Washington, DC 20036
(202) 332-2276 • fax: (202) 332-2949
Web site: www.nccnhr.org

The National Citizens' Coalition for Nursing Home Reform provides information and leadership on federal and state regulatory and legislative policy development and strategies to improve nursing home care and life for residents. The organization also addresses issues such as residents' rights and minimizing the use of physical and chemical restraints. Its publications include the book *Nursing Homes: Getting Good Care There*, NCCNHR's newsletter *Quality Care Advocate*, and fact sheets on issues such as abuse and neglect and how to choose a nursing home.

## National Council on the Aging (NCOA)

300 D St. SW, Suite 801, Washington, DC 20024
(202) 479-1200 • fax: (202) 479-0735
e-mail: info@ncoa.org • Web site: www.ncoa.org

The National Council on the Aging is an association of organizations and professionals dedicated to promoting the dignity, self-determination, well-being, and contributions of older persons. It advocates business practices, societal attitudes, and public policies that promote vital aging. NCOA's quarterly magazine *Journal of the National Council on the Aging* provides tools and insights for community service organizations.

**National Institute of Neurological Disorders and Stroke**
NIH Neurological Institute, PO Box 5801, Bethesda, MD 20824
(800) 352-9424
Web site: www.ninds.nih.gov

The mission of the National Institute of Neurological Disorders and Stroke is to reduce the burden of neurological disease on society. The organization's Web site provides information about current research projects as well as current news on neurological disorders.

**National Institute on Aging (NIA)**
Bldg. 31, Rm. 5C27, 31 Center Dr., MSC 2292, Bethesda, MD 20892
Web site: www.nia.nih.gov

The National Institute on Aging, one of the twenty-five institutes and centers of the National Institutes of Health, spearheads a scientific effort to understand the nature of aging and to extend the healthy, active years of life. Its mission is to improve the health and well-being of older Americans through research. Publications available through the NIA include fact sheets, booklets, and *Connections* newsletter.

# BIBLIOGRAPHY

## Books

Ruth Abraham
*When Words Have Lost Their Meaning: Alzheimer's Patients Communicate Through Art.* Westport, CT: Praeger, 2005.

Karen Bellenir, ed.
*Alzheimer's Disease Sourcebook: Basic Consumer Health Information About Alzheimer's Disease, Other Dementias and Related Disorders.* Detroit: Omnigraphics, 2003.

Gayatri Devi
*What Your Doctor May Not Tell You About Alzheimer's Disease: The Complete Guide to Preventing, Treating and Coping with Memory Loss.* New York: Warner, 2004.

Brian Draper
*Dealing with Dementia: A Guide to Alzheimer's Disease and Other Dementias.* Crows Nest, NSW, Australia: Allen & Unwin, 2004.

Judith Levine
*Do You Remember Me? A Father, a Daughter, and a Search for Self.* New York: Free Press, 2004.

William Joel Meggs
*The Inflammation Cure: How to Combat the Hidden Factor Behind Heart Disease, Arthritis, Asthma, Diabetes, Alzheimer's Disease, Osteoporosis, and Other Diseases of Aging.* Chicago: Contemporary Books, 2004.

Judah L. Ronch and Joseph A. Goldfield, eds.
*Mental Wellness in Aging: Strengths-Based Approaches.* Baltimore: Health Professions, 2003.

Marcin Sadowski
*100 Questions and Answers About Alzheimer's Disease.* Sudbury, MA: Jones & Bartlett, 2004.

Eileen Shamy
*A Guide to the Spiritual Dimension of Care for People with Alzheimer's Disease and Related Dementia: More than Body, Brain and Breath.* New York: J. Kingsley, 2003.

William Rodman Shankle
*Preventing Alzheimer's: Prevent, Detect, Diagnose, Treat and Even Halt Alzheimer's Disease and Other Causes of Memory Loss.* New York: G.P. Putnam's Sons, 2004.

## Periodicals

Thomas D. Bird
"Genetic Factors in Alzheimer's Disease," *New England Journal of Medicine*, March 3, 2005.

Judith R. Brindle
"Meeting the Challenge of Alzheimer's Care," *RN*, January 2005.

Stacey Builing
"Cancer Drug May Have Effect on Alzheimer's," *Knight Ridder Tribune Business News*, December 21, 2004.

Christel Cornelius
"Drug Use in the Elderly: Risk or Protection?" *Current Opinion in Psychiatry*, November 2004.

Alice Dembner
"Descending into Violence; Assaults by Residents with Dementia Pose a Problem for Assisted Living Facilities," *Boston Globe*, May 16, 2004.

| | |
|---|---|
| *Drug Week* | "Alzheimer's Disease: Cholesterol-Lowering Statin Drugs Emerge as Having Alzheimer's Application," October 22, 2004. |
| Kathleen Fackelmann | "Drugs for Alzheimer's Agitation Often Ineffective, Study Says: Antidepressants, Mood Stabilizers Not Designed for Older Patients," *USA Today*, February 2, 2005. |
| Victor W. Henderson and Terri Edwards-Lee | "Diagnosis and Treatment of Alzheimer's Disease," *Journal of Clinical Outcomes Management*, January 2005. |
| Scott Hensley | "Spinal Tap Can Spot Alzheimer's," *Wall Street Journal*, December 15, 2004. |
| Bonnie Liebman | "Fading Memories: The Heart-Weight Connection," *Nutrition Action Health Letter*, January/February 2005. |
| *Obesity, Fitness and Wellness Week* | "Alzheimer's Disease: Researchers Turn to Brain Power to Beat Dementia," March 12, 2005. |
| Andrea Peterson | "New Treatments for Alzheimer's Symptoms: To Curb Aggression, Paranoia in Dementia Patients, Doctors Turn to Schizophrenia Drugs," *Wall Street Journal*, August 26, 2004. |
| Sarah Ringold | "Gene Vaccination to Bias the Immune Response to Amyloid-beta Peptide as Therapy for Alzheimer's Disease," *JAMA*, February 2, 2005. |
| Phillip E. Ross | "Managing Care Through the Air," *IEEE Spectrum*, December 2004. |
| Richard Sadovsky | "Long-Term Care of Patients with Alzheimer's Disease," *American Family Physician*, February 1, 2005. |
| *Science Letter* | "Alzheimer's Disease: Drugs Used to Treat AD in Nursing Homes Are Worsening Illness," March 15, 2005. |
| *Scientific American* | "Downsized Target," May 2004. |
| Katherine Seligman | "The Broken Family Tree: How Bea Gorman's Sad Family History of Alzheimer's Provides Researchers with Fodder for Years of Work," *San Francisco Chronicle*, November 14, 2004. |
| Kylie Taggart | "New Drug Treats Moderate to Severe Alzheimer's Disease," *Medical Post*, January 4, 2005. |
| David Wahlberg | "New Data Connect Two Diseases; Alzheimer's, Diabetes Link Divides Scientists," *Atlanta Journal-Constitution*, March 7, 2005. |
| Catharine Wang, Richard Gonzales, and Sofia D. Merajver | "Assessment of Genetic Testing and Related Counseling Services: Current Research and Future Directions," *Social Science and Medicine*, April 2004. |
| Linda Zinn | "Unlocking What Remains," *Nursing Homes*, February 2005. |

# INDEX